Why Fight Poverty?

PERSPECTIVES

Series editor: Diane Coyle

Why Fight Poverty?

Julia Unwin

LONDON PUBLISHING PARTNERSHIP

Published by London Publishing Partnership
www.londonpublishingpartnership.co.uk

ISBN: 978-1-907994-16-6 (pbk.)

A catalogue record for this book is
available from the British Library

This book has been composed in Candara

Copy-edited and typeset by
T&T Productions Ltd, London

Cover design: Kate Prentice

Contents

Preface

The fight against poverty in the United Kingdom has become at the same time both angry and fruitless.

Despite a historic and continuing concern, there is no shared understanding or perspective on poverty, its causes or its solutions. Interventions to reduce poverty have been piecemeal, poorly understood and have rarely had the sense of shared endeavour and commitment that are central to success.

In this book, I argue that we urgently need to resolve poverty, because it is costly, wasteful and risky – and that we can do so.

Emotions normally have little place in works of either social policy or economics. Such books pride themselves on rigorous analysis, careful diagnosis and thoughtful prescription. This book acknowledges the important contribution of these disciplines but does something different. It focuses on the sentiment and the emotional responses that shape thinking about poverty and inequality and provide such powerful obstacles to effective response.

Attempts to end poverty have foundered, partly because they are not supported by the public. Why? Because powerful emotions get in the way: shame, fear, disgust, difference and mistrust are created and reinforced by our attitudes to poverty and the stories we tell about it.

I argue that our efforts to tackle poverty have been impeded by the political right's tendency to focus on individual agency – people's capacity to act independently and make their own free choices – and the political left's tendency to focus on structural overhaul – in other words, changing the systems and structures that govern society, including taxes, benefits and services. This political stalemate has shaped a widespread public belief that poverty is inevitable.

I dispute this belief that current levels of poverty in the United Kingdom are acceptable and inevitable. They can be reduced.

Those concerned about poverty are decried as almost automatically politically motivated, with a hard-wired assumption that anyone concerned about poverty must, by definition, be left wing. And yet as soon as people of any political persuasion, or none, join the debate, a further false polarization is created: poverty is either seen as simply a product of social and economic structure, or conversely as solely a matter of individual choice and circumstance.

In the resulting barrage of noise and argument, the damage caused by poverty to individuals, families and communities and to wider society is easily overlooked.

This creates a stalemate. Reducing the levels of state support to people in poverty is politically popular. This in turn justifies a focus on only this aspect of relieving poverty. Anxiety about the lifestyles of individuals and families becomes the stuff of salacious and highly critical descriptions of a life in poverty, adopting preconceived positions and ignoring both the experience of people who are poor and the evidence about what their lives are really like.

Attempts to fight poverty rapidly descend into heated argument, shedding little light and resolving nothing. What is more, this stalemate leaves people facing just the same risk of poverty, and just the same challenges in overcoming it. It ensures that both political leadership and administrative effort are noisily diverted from the task of developing a 'social contract' fit for the twenty-first century that allows people to maximize their potential.

A social contract is a settlement between the people and the state. It describes what people can expect of each other, of market and community institutions and of the state. This set of expectations creates a framework that aims to improve lives for everyone's benefit.

We will not make sustained progress on reducing poverty, though, until we acknowledge our own attitudes and value people who are in poverty.

We can only create a strong, shared understanding of poverty and how to end it when we recognize that 'they' are people like 'us'. Looking at individual agency and structural change separately will not achieve the change we need – we must address both together.

Acknowledgements

This Perspective has been shaped and informed by the work of the Joseph Rowntree Foundation and the Joseph Rowntree Housing Trust and their shared long-term commitment to use evidence from research and experience to influence lasting social change.

The book would not have been completed without the encouragement of Abigail Scott Paul, the skilled and patient editing of Paul Brook and, above all, the diligent and supportive research done by Beth Hurrell, who must take huge credit for the thorough application of evidence and the distillation of so many disparate pieces of research. I am also grateful to enlightened economist Diane Coyle who prompted me to write this. Thanks also go to Emma Stone, Chris Goulden and Aleks Collingwood. As ever any errors and mistakes are all mine.

Chapter 1

Introduction:
why fight poverty?

People have been concerned about high levels of poverty for centuries, and that concern has been expressed in various ways throughout history.

Anxiety about how 'the feral' and 'the untamed poor' behave has jostled uneasily with a concern for morality, competed with a sense of shame, and even co-habited with guilt at the existence of hardship in a wealthy country.

The real nature of poverty has always been disputed and there has been a strong and compelling narrative about how personal character keeps people in poverty.

Persistently, through this age-old concern, there has been a desire to tackle and end it. Sometimes that desire has been expressed through a conviction that a free market will eventually lift everyone to at least a tolerable level. At other times it has taken the form of confidence in the abilities of individuals, charity or the state to achieve change.

But despite our continued efforts, poverty persists. This book explores this historic concern and how it has changed. It suggests that frequently it is our emotional responses and the stories we tell about poverty that stop us tackling it effectively.

Poverty and welfare reform

The current debate about poverty in the United Kingdom (Figure 1.1) is almost entirely dominated by welfare reform, a loose term for changes in how the state provides financial support for people who cannot support themselves. The social security system is important but it is not the whole story. This political debate about how to support people in a fair and comprehensible manner gets in the way of a larger truth.

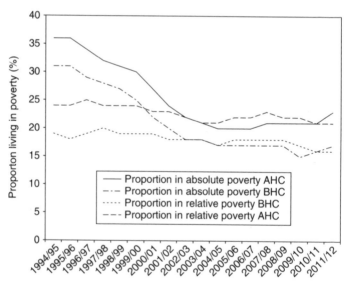

Figure 1.1. Proportion of people living in absolute and relative poverty before and after housing costs (BHC and AHC). *Source*: Households Below Average Income, Department for Work and Pensions (figures are for Great Britain up to 2001/02 and for the United Kingdom thereafter).

For research shows that poverty is neither overcome by welfare, nor caused by it. The structure of society, the choices made and how money is allocated are much more significant in the long term. We know that offering £4bn to low-income families will not be enough to meet the child poverty target without also taking into account employment, training, education, childcare and so on.[1]

Assumptions and assertions about social security blind us to the real questions about poverty:

- How does a good society cope with the fact that some people do not have enough to meet their needs?
- What methods are most effective and what outcomes are acceptable?
- Where does the responsibility lie and who pays for it?

The focus on welfare has a long and enduring history. The Elizabethan Poor Law's principle of 'less eligibility' stipulated that the pauper's condition inside the workhouse should be less attractive than the poorest labourer's situation outside the workhouse, otherwise poorer people would simply choose not to work. This principle continues, largely unquestioned, to this very day in attitudes towards poor and long-term unemployed people, the long-term unemployed and those on welfare. It is rooted in pragmatic (cost) concerns and deep emotional responses including shame, fear, disgust, mistrust and envy.

The only disagreement is about how minimal the provision for a life without work should be. The objective – 'making work pay' – that surrounds the debate over welfare reform policies is a twenty-first-century version of the long-standing idea that the only spur for poor people to work is the threat of even greater poverty if they do not. Benefit sanctions serve the same apparent objective. Whether they work to drive behaviour, or only result in 'poor job matches, lower wages and higher turnover',[2] is a matter for loud political debate, but only occasionally the subject of careful analysis.

The welfare system undoubtedly needs massive reform. It has been criticized for trapping people in poverty and for demeaning those it seeks to help, and it is complex and expensive. In 2011–12 over £200 billion (or 13.5 per cent of GDP) was spent on social security benefits. This includes:

- £36,998m of benefits for families with children;
- £5,164m for unemployed people;
- £41,811m for people on low incomes;
- £85,011m for elderly people;
- £31,215m for disabled people; and
- £623m for bereaved people.[3]

The system is not fit for purpose, and it will need to adapt as we live longer and need more care. In an ever more volatile labour market, with changing family structures and working patterns, we need a more secure and flexible welfare system.

However, the current approach to reforming the system is piecemeal and frequently poorly evidenced. The cumulative effect is risky for individuals as well as the local and national economy. The development of Universal Credit is a welcome and potentially very important way of ensuring that people can cope with a fluctuating labour market. However, there are well-founded concerns about the ways it is to be implemented and the impact of the tapers. Research carried out before the implementation of Universal Credit reveals the risks of changing to monthly single payments and highlights the need for clarity over financial support.[4]

The move towards engaging with people mainly online will need sustained support. Changes to Working Tax Credits, Housing Benefit and many other benefits, along with caps on benefit uprating, will create significant social upheaval and hardship for individuals and communities.[5]

INTRODUCTION: WHY FIGHT POVERTY?

Furthermore, of course the role of welfare needs exam-
ination, but if we think poverty can be relieved by welfare
alone we are missing the point. Poverty is much more complex and challenging than that. More than half of children and
working-age adults in poverty are in working households,[6] so
while work is undoubtedly a way out of poverty for some, low
pay and irregular hours mean that working poverty is a visible
feature of our times (Figure 1.2). We will need to change how
labour is rewarded, the type of work, opportunities for progression, stability and number of hours, as well as the cost of
housing, food, fuel, childcare and other essentials.

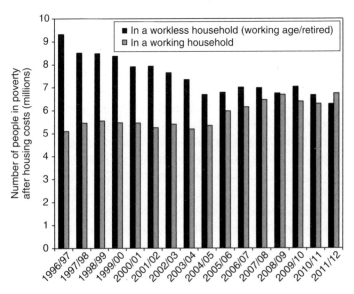

Figure 1.2. In-work poverty. *Source*: Households Below Average Income,
Department for Work and Pensions (figures are for Great Britain).

We need a much better understanding of how we support
each other, and how money – and other support – is passed

around in communities and within families before we can think about reducing poverty. We need to understand the very different experiences of poverty, and how gender, disability and ill health all influence someone's chances of becoming poor. We need to know more about the role of culture, attitude and behaviour in shaping people's experience of poverty.

During difficult times of labour market uncertainty, housing market volatility and increasing costs, we must not confuse the need for a well-designed social security system with the changes needed to end poverty.

Hard times

The global financial crisis of 2008 changed the United Kingdom dramatically. It is still too early to gauge quite how profound that change has been and what its long-term effects will be. The financial disaster was followed by a period of austerity and a government determined to reduce the deficit, with a relentless focus on the national debt, and a prevailing view that expenditure had to be reduced. Economists have promised little in the way of recovery. While a triple-dip recession has been avoided, there seems little prospect of a return to rapid sustainable growth in the foreseeable future.

Public spending cuts and the lack of growth in the economy are not the only reasons this is a tough time for people in poverty. The labour market is going through a major restructure and the resulting insecurity at the lower end of the market is creating a different sort of job offer.

Jobs are more short term than ever, with rapid movement between low-paid work and unemployment.[7] Short-term or zero hours contracts, unreliable and variable hours and a big increase in casual labour are the hallmarks of a labour market that offers neither security nor progression. Equally, the growth of self-employment to 13 per cent, occasionally heralded as the resurgence of a new form of enterprise, may be revealed[8] as simply a different form of casual labour.

There is a long-term trend of polarization in the job market, with more highly paid jobs and more low-paid jobs, but fewer and fewer in the middle. This makes it harder for people at the bottom of the labour market to progress into better-paid work (Figure 1.3) and can lead to some working below their skill level, making it even more difficult for those without qualifications to find jobs.[9]

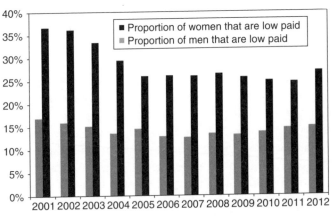

Figure 1.3. Low pay over time. *Source*: Annual Survey of Hours and Earnings, Office for National Statistics (figures are for the United Kingdom).

The boundary between graduate and non-graduate work is becoming increasingly blurred. As more graduates enter the job market, they are increasingly taking jobs that were traditionally 'non-graduate'. The percentage of graduates earning below the hourly wage has risen over the past 15 years, while the number earning above the hourly wage fell from 47.9 per cent in 1993 to 23.1 per cent in 2008.[10]

There has also been persistent exploitation in some sectors, particularly those characterized by long supply chains or demand for cheap labour.[11] There is evidence that forced labour occurs in a number of sectors in the United Kingdom and often involves difficult, dirty and dangerous work, alongside threats or actual violence towards workers, and cramped, expensive accommodation. Migrant workers in particular are vulnerable to forced labour situations at the extreme end of a murky labour market.

In this context the government can intervene in the labour market to regulate employment or it can subsidize low-paid workers to enable subsistence. The alternative of doing neither results in people working without sufficient means to maintain themselves and their families.

The housing market is the second great contributor to high levels of poverty. Five per cent or 3.1 million more people experienced poverty in 2010–11 when housing costs had been taken into account.[12] The United Kingdom housing market is as volatile as ever, with rising costs in London and the South-East and considerable pockets of decline elsewhere.

And with new caps to Local Housing Allowance, housing has become even less affordable. In 34 per cent of local authorities in England, the maximum Local Housing Allowance was not enough to cover the cheapest quarter of two-bedroom rents.[13] London and the east of England had the highest proportion of local authorities where housing was largely unaffordable (17 out of 32 London boroughs and 8 out of 20 in the east of England).[13] The costs of renting rose 3.5 per cent in May 2013 (7.2 per cent in London) and the average rent reached £737 in England and Wales.[14]

The third in this trinity of markets is the cost of essential items such as fuel, food, finance, council tax, domestic heating and power, transport and insurance. In 2012, these costs increased by 3.7 per cent, much faster than Consumer Price Index inflation. At the same time, nominal income growth was 1.6 per cent. Most significantly, wages have stagnated and costs of essentials have increased since 2008. JRF's Minimum Income Standards research shows the cost of living has increased by 25 per cent since 2008.[15] This has put particular pressure on low-income groups.[16]

In short, we have a more or less flat-lining economy, an increasingly polarized labour market and a highly regionalized, localized housing market, combined with stagnating pay and a rapidly increasing cost of living.

Although the context is difficult, the impact on the poorest people and places does not need to be so harsh.

In our recent past, in the wake of world wars, we have built housing, invested in our infrastructure and developed free health care to sit alongside our free education. Shared endeavour has resulted in substantial change.

We could forge a new, more resilient social contract, to commit to tackling poverty and ensuring the provision of a safety net for us all.

This is not happening at the moment. The National Centre for Social Research's analysis of the British Social Attitudes surveys shows that attitudes towards people in poverty are increasingly unsympathetic.

In 2010, 23 per cent believed poverty was caused by character weakness or behaviour, compared to 15 per cent in 1994. This view was particularly strong among people aged over 65.[17] The number of people who perceived social injustices to be the main cause of poverty decreased from 29 per cent in 1994 to 21 per cent in 2010.[18] In 2011 two-thirds of people blamed parents' behaviour and characters as the main cause of child poverty.[19] At the same time, support for welfare spending has decreased, particularly among 18–24 year olds.

There is currently no shared belief or understanding about poverty and no shared endeavour to solve it.

Many people believe that poverty does not exist in the United Kingdom or that it does not matter – deeply held views that accord with their experience. Any attempt to address rising levels of poverty needs to understand these views, and take them very seriously indeed.

Does poverty exist in the United Kingdom?

In 2009, 39 per cent of people thought there was 'very little' real poverty in the United Kingdom and many strongly dispute the suggestion that it exists (Figure 1.4).[20]

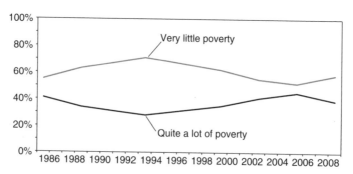

Figure 1.4. Public perceptions of the level of poverty in Britain.
Source: British Social Attitudes Survey, NatCen.

They argue that while there is real poverty in other countries, any poverty in the United Kingdom is less severe, and describing it as such is misleading and untruthful.

They are right to some extent. There is a world of difference between UK poverty in 2013 and 100 years ago, just as poverty in a village in Africa with no electricity and an absolute shortage of water and food is different from someone in Scotland living in a damp, poorly maintained home with insufficient to pay for their bus fare. There is also a world of difference in wealth. The middle-class homeowner of the 1920s would not understand or comprehend the income, assets and choices of their counterpart in the twenty-first century. Measurement of income and wealth are inevitably relative – and they are so regardless of the level of income or wealth.

All poverty is relative and needs to be seen in context. Needs are relative in every society and differ depending on the price of food and other goods, and social norms – the opportunity to participate in society, e.g. buying birthday presents for family members or social activities for children.

To fulfil these needs, people mainly need money, but also other formal resources, such as health services and education, and informal resources, such as informal childcare, borrowing money from a friend and so on.

The resources someone needs can change over time and vary between people and places, depending on the range, sustainability, quantity and quality of their resources, individual and family circumstances, and the choices people make. Because UK poverty is relative, it can be easier to ignore or dismiss – but it is real and affects a sizeable portion of our population, with implications for our whole society.

Chapter 2

Does poverty matter?

There is a strong belief in some quarters that poverty is not really important at all. In any competitive and successful society, it is argued, there are some who will do better than others, which means that some will do much worse. Poverty is an inevitable by-product of our largely prosperous and successful economy, and, by and large, people of skill and determination will get themselves out of poverty.

There are others who believe that poverty does matter, but only for the individual and not for society, so any attempts to change the odds or interfere with people's choices are unnecessary and unhelpful distortions to a market economy.

Sitting alongside these views is the frequently expressed belief that poverty's continuing existence actually provides some benefit. It gives a dire warning of an alternative future so spurs people on to more effort.

More subtly, the debate revolves around how much political effort is needed to reduce poverty, and whether it deserves it. The issue at stake is whether poverty is some private, individual misfortune or a much wider, societal issue. C. Wright Mills describes it as follows:

> When, in a city of 100,000, only one man is unemployed, that is his personal trouble, and for its relief we properly look to

the character of the man, his skills, and his immediate opportunities. But when in a nation of 50 million employees, 15 million men are unemployed, that is an issue, and we may not hope to find its solution within the range of opportunities open to any one individual.[21]

The belief that poverty does not matter for society is linked with the belief that intervention may create a mollycoddled, dependent population, incapable of motivation and ambition. This is an increasingly prevalent attitude. In 2011, 54 per cent believed that if benefits were lower, people would stand on their own two feet, an increase from 33 per cent in 1987 (Figure 2.1).[22] The argument is that someone's ability to rise above their circumstances in life is the only answer to poverty, and, in a well-functioning free market, the clever and able will rise, and make provision for their own.

There have been enduring challenges to these views, however. Many politicians, philanthropists, practitioners and members of the public have long advocated that poverty not only exists meaningfully in the United Kingdom but that it also matters both for individuals and for society.

For centuries, reformers have argued – in different ways and from different perspectives – that there are hard-headed, pragmatic reasons for fighting poverty. They have pointed to the waste of human potential, and the opportunities lost by allowing people to remain in penury. They have argued too that those without sufficient income are unable to participate in an economy that requires consumption. They have identified the costs associated with high levels of poverty, noting the long-term costs to the economy of people and places blighted in this way. And they have noted the risks to our shared society of people whose lack of income effectively forces them to live outside social norms. Waste,

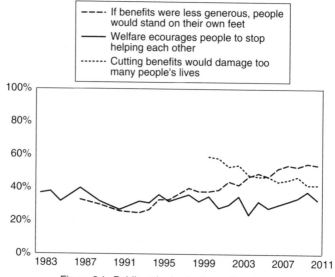

Figure 2.1. Public attitudes to the welfare state.
Source: British Social Attitudes Survey, NatCen.

cost and risk are balance-sheet concerns that have been documented by social reformers of all stripes, motivations and political persuasions.

Joseph Rowntree, a Quaker and industrialist, argued that the causes of poverty were primarily structural.

Seebohm Rowntree's 1899 Study of Town Life examined poverty by surveying the minimum basket of goods and nutrition a household needed in relation to their income. He found that – in a striking parallel with the twenty-first century – over half of those in poverty were also in work.[23]

Beatrice Webb was concerned about the effect of poverty on people's morality and capability. She argued that the Poor Laws resulted in a loss of self-respect and dignity, which increased the persistence of poverty, and further increased expense.[24] The Poor Laws were also ineffective because they focused on individual behaviour, whereas Webb believed the main causes to be structural, or factors beyond individual control, such as illness. The waste of human life was also central in her concern; for example, unnecessarily high infant mortality due to parents entering the workhouse.

Webb advocated universal provision that did not separate destitute people from everyone else. Means testing cost more money and categorizing people was demoralizing and stigmatizing.

William Beveridge argued that unemployment was a problem because it left people without resources, wasted their skills, and, more importantly, left them outside civic life.[25]

He believed that any social contract should be based around mutual solidarity, contractual entitlement, active citizenship and altruism. He supported contributory principles that would help the individual, state and market to work together. Beveridge advocated solutions that would address what he perceived to be the root causes of poverty, while always focusing on the whole population, and resisting efforts to focus only on the poorest. He believed that improving morals without reorganizing industry would fail to create jobs, as 'inadequate character' was largely determined by adverse industrial conditions.[26] He argued that people should always be better off in work than with social security and that any solutions to poverty should not undermine incentives to work. Subsidy would be minimal and there would be controls against fraud and abuse.[27]

All of these pioneering analysts avoided sentimentality. As we have seen from this briefest of overviews, those who wished to eradicate poverty had three main arguments; their concern was with the costs and waste of poverty, and with the risk both for the individual and society. They believed that interventions could reduce these.

Beveridge's predecessors were dismayed when they en-countered rickets-ridden young men incapable of fighting in the Boer War, so they instituted free school meals as a way of overcoming malnutrition. In the same way, we are concerned about the waste of skills, opportunities and creativity that poverty creates today.

The current costs of poverty

Recent research supports the view that poverty squanders human ability, capability and potential.

Pupils eligible for free school meals are almost half as likely to achieve five or more A*–C grades at GCSE compared with those who are not eligible.[28] Figures from the Office for National Statistics reveal that the number of underemployed workers now stands at 3.05 million (2012), a rise of nearly 1 million since 2008 (Figure 2.2). Nearly three-quarters say they want to work more hours in their current job, although this may mean they want to earn more rather than work longer hours.[29] Poverty is wasteful to a country in desperate need of the skills and capacity needed to compete globally.

Kyle, 23, living in a deprived area in Knowsley, unable to find a job despite his enthusiasm:

'The worst thing about it is you start getting used to [not having a job]. Yeah you just get depressed.'

Child poverty costs an esti-mated £29bn a year, which in-cludes public spending to deal with its effects, e.g. the cost of social services, education, police and criminal justice. The £8.5bn of lost earnings to individuals affects GDP and £5.9bn is spent on extra benefits and lower tax revenues for adults who grew up in poverty.[30]

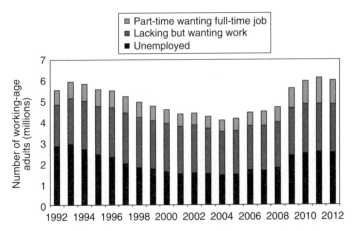

Figure 2.2. Underemployment. *Source*: Labour Market Statistics, Office for National Statistics (figures for the United Kingdom).

Very low-paid work costs us all dear too – in the last couple of decades, tax credits have been needed just to achieve a level of subsistence pay for unreliable work that offers no progression to more secure or well-paid employment.

There is a strong relationship between growing up in poverty and being unemployed or in low-skilled, low-paid jobs in later life, even when background and education are accounted for. There is also a relationship between a childhood in poverty and being poor in later life.[31]

> Dec, a resident and community volunteer on the Marsh Farm estate in Luton:
>
> '[There are] suicidal people [on Jobseeker's Allowance], people with mental health issues, and if they didn't have them, they have them now, because they're being so degraded, so run down in life.'

Disability and poor health are linked to and contribute to poverty. People in families where someone is disabled

17

made up 34 per cent of all people in poverty in 2010–11 (Figure 2.3).[32] Unemployment is strongly related to health – having a health problem that is classed as disabling doubles the level of unemployment to 50 per cent.

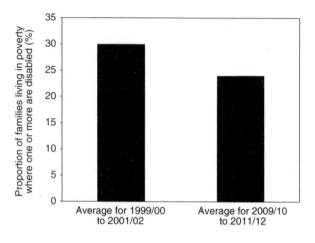

Figure 2.3. Proportion of families living in poverty where someone is disabled. *Source*: Households Below Average Income, Department for Work and Pensions (figures for Great Britain up to 2001/02 and for the United Kingdom thereafter).

Seventy-five per cent of disabled people who have a mental health problem do not work.[33] Of those who can work, there is a higher proportion of low-paid disabled workers than non-disabled workers.[34] Although more research is needed on the links between poverty and mental health (and vice versa), it is clear that 24 per cent of adults in the poorest fifth of the population are likely to be at risk of developing mental health problems, compared with 14 per cent of those on average incomes.[35]

Poverty is also linked to health inequalities that are both costly to society and wasteful of human life (Figure 2.4).

People in the most deprived neighbourhoods live – on average – seven years less than those in the richest neighbourhoods. They spend an average of seventeen years longer with a disability.[36] This amounts to 1.3 million years of life lost (each child could expect to live two years longer).[37]

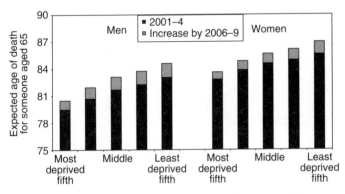

Figure 2.4. Expected age at death at age 65 for men and women. *Source*: Inequality in Disability-Free Life Expectancy by Area Deprivation: England, 2001–05 and 2006–09, Office for National Statistics (May 2012).

These health inequalities carry a significant cost – £31–33 billion of lost productivity per year in addition to lost taxes and higher welfare payments of £20–32 billion per year, plus NHS healthcare costs.[37]

Poverty is strongly associated with offending and antisocial behaviour. Evidence looking at the United States may not transfer directly to the United Kingdom but does indicate that people growing up in deprived areas have a greater chance of being a victim of crime. There is also a strong association between experiencing crime as a victim and becoming an offender.[38] One does not necessarily cause the other, although evidence suggests that poor family functioning and low self-esteem, fuelled by child poverty, can contribute to antisocial behaviour.[39]

Poverty has an enduring and scarring effect across the lives of people who experience it. This varies depending on the persistence and depth of poverty. People in poverty say that it wastes their capability and skills, erodes hope and ambition, and makes it hugely difficult to make long-term plans or move on.

So poverty is costly. *The Poor Pay More*[40] was written forty-five years ago, but in our globalized, internet-enabled world people in poverty now pay so much more. Save the Children estimated in 2007 that poor people pay over £1,280 more for basic goods than better-off families. By 2010 this had increased by another £280.[41]

> Despite an increase of education courses, the poverty in Barkerend lays waste to ability. A youth and community worker says:
>
> 'At the end of it there's nothing [for the young people] and it all seems pointless to them.'[46]

People in poverty pay more for energy by using prepayment meters. It is harder to switch utility companies or shop around for cheaper deals, partly because there are fewer options, or there is limited access to comparison websites if they cannot afford internet access.

People in poverty also find it more difficult to access credit at low cost or at all, so some people turn to doorstep lenders. Anecdotal evidence highlights the reality of this; one family borrowed £500 over a year and paid £400 in interest.[42] People who cannot afford to buy outright may use 'rent to own' retailers and could face total payments much higher than the normal price. For example, a washing machine for sale in BrightHouse, the weekly payment retail company, offering white goods (fridges, freezers, washing machines, etc.) to poorer families can be paid for over 156 weeks at a total cost of £606.84. The same washing machine is available from Sainsbury's for £336.[43]

Changes in council tax benefit in 2013/14 mean that 2.4 million low-income families now pay on average £138 more in council tax as the majority of councils reduce support.[44]

There is also cost and waste for those who live in poor places. Research into two deprived areas in Scotland, Govan in Glasgow and Gallatown in Kirkcaldy, Fife, found that physical deterioration of the areas led to a decline in investment. Long-term planning was difficult because of stagnation in the labour market, and people's hopes and ambitions were eroded because of the limited opportunities in employment, education and housing. There were further losses of knowledge, expertise and networks – for example, in Glasgow nearly 90 voluntary organizations ceased to exist in 2009.[45]

Photograph by Liz Hingley.

Deprived areas have also been most affected by the recent recession, with areas such as the West Midlands and the North-West of England suffering most. Unemployment

21

increased most in communities where it was already highest and these areas remained more disadvantaged after recession hit.[46]

Research into the impact of recession on local authorities found that generally the most deprived authorities made greater spending cuts than the most affluent, both proportionally and in absolute terms.[47] And cuts often affected services like transport or youth services that had a significant impact on the most disadvantaged people.

Poverty brings huge risk too. Instability for people in short-term, low-paid, insecure work creates financial insecurity and increases the risk of not being able to pay rent or bills, or afford essential items. It threatens relationships, erodes ambition and can pit poor people against very poor people, eroding the opportunities for mutual support.

Poverty is harmful, but not just for individuals. It is a public issue. It affects communities and society through the waste, cost and risk it imposes.

So yes, poverty does matter. We should focus our efforts on reducing it and the damage, enduring waste and significant risk it causes for people who experience it – and because of the harm it does to our national balance sheet.

Chapter 3

Why is there little public support for solving poverty?

If poverty matters, why is there so little support for solving it? Some of this lack of support is generated by the very arguments already considered – that poverty does not exist, and that it does not matter.

We respond emotionally to people who are poor and to the question of poverty. A parallel narrative about poverty exists alongside the surface debate. This is a narrative that unearths deep and challenging feelings and both disrupts and distorts the otherwise apparently rational path of social reform. A deep anxiety about vulnerability, weakness and failure is translated into a sense of shame, of fear, of disgust and occasionally anger, which prevents rational discussion.

Feelings of shame, fear, disgust and difference stop us empathizing, reduce our motivation to intervene and get in the way of a shared endeavour to solve poverty. These feelings are created and reinforced by our attitudes and the stories we tell about poverty. Our fear of failure, and of consequent vulnerability, is so profound and deep-seated that it constantly inhibits our ability to act.

Most changes in social policy require public support. We will not be able to create a shared endeavour to solve poverty unless we first understand the nature of our emotional responses.

Our attitudes are affected by what we see and hear in the media, people's stories and testimony, and political debate. These attitudes reveal – and result in – a reduction of public support, and involve myths and generalization, as well as considerable elements of truth. Significant work has been done to increase public support by confronting attitudes and debunking myths, in particular work from the Webb Memorial Trust and the Centre for Labour and Social Studies.

Some of the most prevalent attitudes about poverty

Laziness

In 2010, 23 per cent of the public perceived the main cause of poverty to be laziness or a lack of willpower; an increase from 15 per cent in 1994.[48]

But as we have seen, over half of all children and working-age adults in poverty now live in working households.[6] 'Work is the best route out of poverty' is a half-truth. Only 56 per cent of households stop being poor a year after someone from that household gets a new job.[49]

Much public and political debate has focused on inherited unemployment[50] where there is no work in a couple of generations. Work by Teesside University in deprived Middlesbrough and Glasgow neighbourhoods shows that it is rare to find families where two generations of households have never worked (15,000 households) and even rarer to find any with three generations.[51]

Drugs and alcohol

There is little evidence to support the belief that drug and alcohol dependency is one of the main causes of poverty, despite what is shown in the British Social Attitudes Survey[52] and interpretations of DWP research.[53]

We do not know exactly how many parents in poverty are problem drug or alcohol users, but of those people who receive out-of-work benefits (not necessarily parents) 7 per cent are estimated to be problem drug users and 4 per cent dependent drinkers.[54]

Big families

Despite significant media attention paid to large, poor families, only 8 per cent of benefit claimants have three or more children.[55]

Fraud

Surveys and the tabloid press[56] echo common attitudes that many people receiving Incapacity Benefit and Jobseeker's Allowance are falsely claiming. But overpayments for Incapacity Benefit fraud in 2012–13 were estimated at £10 million, compared with £40 million of official error.[57] In the same year, Jobseeker's Allowance benefits fraud was estimated at £150 million, again compared with £40 million of official error.[57] This is lower than 2011–12 estimates of £32 billion of lost taxes.[58]

These attitudes remain strong. The number of people who feel that more should be spent on benefits has certainly fallen, particularly among 18–24 year olds, where the proportion fell from around 50 per cent in 1987 to 20 per cent in 2011.[59]

To understand why these attitudes persist, and indeed why they are hardening, it is first important to understand the context behind them.

Stories

People have always talked about poverty and worried about what should be done. The persistence of the themes is striking, as is the way poverty is discussed. The cumulated impact of these stories lies at the heart of how we talk and think about poverty today. Stories help many people make the leap of imagination that leads them to want to see poverty reduced – but they compete with the alternative narrative of blame and the impossibility of change.

The major Abrahamic faiths, which are prominent in the United Kingdom, all see the relief of poverty as part of the duty of the faithful, whether they ascribe poverty to bad luck, personal weakness or someone's wrongdoing. The Old Testament books of Exodus, Leviticus and Deuteronomy highlight special provisions for poor people, such as the cancelling of debts in the Sabbatical year and the stipulation that those who could not afford to offer a sacrificial lamb could instead offer two pigeons, or even something smaller.

The New Testament presents a more challenging perspective – contrasting those with wealth directly against poor people, and making the case for the rich man to sacrifice what he has if he is to secure eternal salvation.

In more recent times, the stories we tell and are told – far more than the facts – play a major role in shaping attitudes and political decisions. In the United Kingdom and the United States, there is a rich tradition of storytelling and novel writing as a form of social protest. Our literature is full of stories and characters that have moulded attitudes to poverty.

Charles Dickens conjured up a world of people living in poverty with full and rounded characters: orphans and debtors, impoverished gentry and child labourers.

Thomas Hardy depicted grinding rural poverty, seduction, illegitimacy and class exclusion. Novels were credited with extraordinary political powers – Harriet Beecher Stowe in *Uncle Tom's Cabin* is reported to have 'Lit a million camp fires in front of the embattled hosts of slavery.'[60]

Uncle Tom's Cabin invigorated the abolition movement in a way that mere factual evidence had not. This was not an isolated example of fiction having an influence on popular perceptions of social ills.

Upton Sinclair in *The Jungle* illuminated the horrors of working practices, and *The Grapes of Wrath* made real the experience of indentured travelling labour (a form of debt bondage).

In *The Road to Wigan Pier*, George Orwell was a storyteller visiting another world. Using journalistic as well as novelistic skill he reported the poverty he discovered in hidden places.

Walter Greenwood's *Love on the Dole* described the waste of youth unemployment, unfulfilled ambition and potential and the harshness of the means test.

Alan Sillitoe vividly described the isolation, lack of opportunity and resort to crime in *Loneliness of the Long Distance Runner*.

Seminal work like Jeremy Seabrook's *Cathy Come Home* shook a generation in the mid-60s, inspiring an increase in charitable activity and many supporters of the newly formed Shelter – and, shortly after, the Notting Hill Housing Trust – while Nell Dunn in *Up the Junction* wrote passionately about the reality of life for poor women in South London.

These works and many more described poverty in a way that was meaningful, accessible, and above all respectful. Time and again, reports from the front line, written by people who were themselves rarely poor but had chosen to live alongside those in poverty, painted a picture of the complexity of poverty, populating their stories with real experience and with some depth.

Storytelling changes attitudes in a number of distinctive ways:

- by creating identity with the reader, there is space to develop empathy;
- through the narrative, the story is developed of how the structure of society interacts with the individual;
- as in all stories, there is room for redemption, and therefore there is room for optimism or a sense of change.

Storytelling in this way shapes and influences. It is rare that it transforms attitudes completely, but even a cursory glance at the impact of some of the books mentioned here demonstrates how attitudes are shaped and affected.

Storytelling takes things that would otherwise be obscured and makes them real.

The readers of the novels described here have space to develop empathy, to understand the predicament, and to imagine themselves within it. They will identify the structural forces that create poverty: the legal system in Dickensian London and the approach to debt, the collapse of employment in Orwellian Wigan, the nature of land ownership and casual work in Steinbeck's United States. They will also be able to identify where inevitably human frailty, foolishness or bad behaviour have contributed to that predicament.

The poverty feels real, the environment compelling but crucially there is also room for change and escape. Rescue comes in various forms: inheritance and the rediscovery of family connections in Dickens, marriage in the work of the Brontës and Jane Austen, and the ever-present prospect of a surprise fortune being discovered.

Modern-day literature continues to convey some of the complexity of poverty.

In Monica Ali's *Brick Lane* there is a vivid, empathetic portrayal of the experience of immigration – the disappointment and the hardship, but also the excitement.

More recently, Karen Campbell's *This Is Where I Am* created a picture of the experience of a refugee and his child in modern-day Glasgow. Similarly, *Pigeon English* by Stephen Kelman explored the territory of difference and exclusion and of the enormous vulnerability to random violence.

Kerry Hudson's *Tony Hogan Bought Me an Ice-cream Float before He Stole Me Ma* explores experiences of childhood poverty, neglect and drug abuse and the persistence of chaotic experiences in adulthood, while Lisa O'Donnell's *The Death of Bees*, both murder mystery and social commentary set on a Glasgow housing estate, covers similar themes.

Cloudstreet by Tim Winton chronicles eccentric working-class families in Australia. There are other more extreme stories, such as Irvine Welsh's *Trainspotting*, which gave form, and some would say glamour, among the compellingly foul scenes, to the chaos of drug dependency, squalor, theft and violence.

Non-fiction works reflect some of these themes yet tell a very different story to the one of empathy or redemption. Owen Jones's *Chavs* describes modern-day society as scathingly dismissive of all but the most materially successful, treating a huge swathe of society with contempt, and frequently disgust. Those who labour hard and earn little receive as much contempt as those who 'choose not to work' in a stereotype that equates low income with dependency, and ascribes base motives to all who fail to reach the top of an increasingly disunited society. In Jones's narrative, this dissonance has been driven by the collapse of trade union power and other forms of working-class solidarity and joint action. It has eroded the distinction between 'the working poor' and the rest. In doing so, it has further demonized all who are poor, and ensured that fear and disgust dominate over pity or any sense of empathy.

Shirkers and scroungers

The more prominent recent narrative portrays people in poverty as shirkers or scroungers.

Shameless, a popular UK and US TV fiction series, illustrates the story of 'the problem poor'. There is no differentiation within the group, nor is an alternative 'respectable poor' depicted. The series revolves around the Gallagher family, who lead chaotic and often destructive lives on the fictitious 'Chatsworth council estate' in Manchester. The family live on benefits and Frank Gallagher, neglectful father of six, who has experienced a broken marriage, is an alcoholic and a drug user. The '*Shameless* culture' is often used to describe poor families who lead chaotic lives, often involving antisocial behaviour, violence and abuse of the welfare system. The *Shameless* narrative is told affectionately, but dismissively. There is no suggestion that wider structural change might have had an impact on the lives of the Gallaghers, but more a depiction of them as feckless architects of their own fate, failing to take opportunities, and living a life of relative ease.

Even documentaries that aim to give a realistic picture often do little to present a balanced story and have been criticized by those living in these communities. A Panorama documentary set on the Shadsworth estate in Blackburn, one of the most deprived areas in the country, focused on just a few families and portrayed it as a place where drug abuse, crime and unemployment were widespread. One example showed a lone mother of four children who hadn't worked for eight years. The children had difficulty staying in school due to antisocial behaviour and the mother, a drug user, said 'there's no incentive for getting back to work, it's just a headache'.[42]

Other documentaries, such as *Skint*, which focuses on the West Cliff estate in Scunthorpe, reveal similar vices. Examining just a few families, it covers issues of truancy, drug-taking, children being taken into care, shoplifting and prostitution. One man, a step-father of five children and father of two, casually buys stolen food and says 'there's nowt else to do up here but breed and feed'. Another says 'most people sign on... or sell drugs'.

In these stories the families are depicted as 'the problem poor', living in broken communities. They are to blame for their poverty. If they are truly poor at all, it is because they are lazy and choose not to go out to work. For subsistence they often claim benefits dishonestly or illegally. Their lifestyles cause disruption to those around them and they are a financial burden on society.

Side by side there are stories that manage to illustrate both pity and paternalism, such as *Secret Millionaire* and *How the Other Half Live*, which show wealthy, benevolent people helping those in poverty who are shown as victims of structural injustice.

The popularity of these differing stories demonstrates just how much poverty has become a spectator sport. It reinforces the division between 'them' and 'us'. And the vilification in social media (especially Twitter) of the people in these stories, particularly documentaries such as *Skint*, reveals their impact.

It is vital that these stories are not simply dismissed. Clear and honest counterarguments are vital, but so too is a recognition of the depth and strength of these competing narratives.

We need to understand the impact these attitudes have on public support, and to acknowledge the elements of truth within them.

Most importantly, we must understand the emotions that lie behind these stories and attitudes, and what solutions they lead us to advocate.

The fact is, through malevolent intent or benign ignorance, there are powerful stereotypes at play – and not just from broadcasters. These stories reflect and amplify powerful emotions. They illustrate precisely the anxieties that people have when poverty is discussed, and it is not surprising that these age-old anecdotes come to dominate public and private debate.

Shame, fear, disgust, difference and mistrust

The combined narratives in literature and public policy illustrate remarkably consistent feelings of shame, fear, disgust and difference expressed by and about poor people and poverty, which both contradict and reinforce each other.

The language changes, as does the style, but the messages continue to resonate. Robert Walker has written compellingly about the prevalence of shame as a defining feature of how poor people across the globe view their position. Society also reinforces the feeling of shame, which poor people in turn perceive society to feel about them.

People who could not provide adequate housing and food for themselves or their family felt ashamed, but there was an even stronger sense of shame if people felt unable to live up to expectations.

> Despite respondents generally believing that they had done their best against all odds, they mostly considered that they had both failed themselves for being poor and that others saw them as failures. This internalisation of shame was further externally reinforced in the family, the workplace and in their dealings with officialdom.[61]

People often felt shame because of how they felt they were treated. This often reinforced the shame they already felt. People also felt ashamed when they had to admit their poverty so that they could access services or support. These feelings have been reported elsewhere:

> When you go down to the benefits office you've got to leave your dignity in your back pocket just to get what you're entitled to.[61]

A MORI survey in May 2012 found that 46 per cent of people interviewed felt a high level of institutional stigma (a stigma that arises from the process of claiming benefits). This was significantly higher than the percentage of those who felt personal stigma (a person's own feeling that claiming benefits is shameful) or social stigma (feeling that other people judge claiming benefits to be shameful and conferring a lower social status), which were 8–10 per cent and 11–13 per cent respectively.[62]

Walker found that other common responses from people in poverty were depression, withdrawal from social life and anger. There was a strong sense of the need to keep up appearances, which related to a fear of being 'outed'.[63]

Shame can also be described as pride unmasked, for there is a stigma in not participating fully in society, and this is also linked to a fear of being marked out as different:

> Parents bought branded clothing regardless of their financial wellbeing, to avoid their children being taunted; paradoxically, this shows the importance of the non-material side of poverty, and the powerful threat of labelling or 'othering' of children for signs of difference.[64]

Walker also noted how people felt resigned to their fate, resulting in a decline of motivation, confidence and esteem. He indicates that policies that stigmatize benefit recipients could be counterproductive, as they might contribute to longer periods of poverty. The research revealed that feelings of shame made poor people create a distinction between themselves and an 'other' – the undeserving poor people, who were poor because of a 'lack of trying' as opposed to an 'absence of opportunity'.[65] By trying to remove this shame by creating divisions, people in poverty found a sense of comfort in not being 'the lowest' in society.

It is also striking that the television programme that has, perhaps, done so much to depict a particular caricature of poverty in the United Kingdom is called *Shameless* – a title suggesting it is the lack of shame that is problematic.

Shame has always been used as a powerful way of managing demand for support. The management of the Elizabethan workhouse, later the Victorian Charity Organisation Society, and the various systems of social security in the twentieth century all used shame to some degree to manage demand and ration resources.[66]

These systems relied on shame as a way of ensuring that only those desperate enough would be willing to claim benefit. They minimized any sense of entitlement, emphasized the shame of receiving charity and instilled a sense of gratitude.

The Elizabethan principle of 'less eligibility' sought to ensure that charitable donations were not used by those who did not really require them, and this remains a cornerstone of thinking, relying heavily on shame as a means of policing. Workhouse life was deliberately so grim, and admission so shameful, that only those truly in need would use it.

Thomas Hobbes believed it was in people's interests to have a shared endeavour that provided for individuals as part of a shared social contract. Charity was therefore a failure of this and a cause of shame and stigma:

> Whereas many men ... become unable to maintain themselves by their labour; they ought not to be left to the Charity of private persons; but to be provided for... by the Lawes of the Common-wealth. For as it is Uncharitableness in any man to neglect the impotent; so it is in the Sovereign of a Common-Wealth to expose them to the hazard of such uncertain charity.[67]

Studies of Adam Smith's work reveal his belief that poverty is 'a cause of social isolation and psychic unease' rather than a 'condition of economic deprivation'.[68] Poverty is relative and related to shame:

> The Greeks and Romans lived, I suppose, very comfortably though they had no linen. But in the present times, through the greater part of Europe, a creditable day-labourer would be ashamed to appear in public without a linen shirt, the want of which would be supposed to denote that disgraceful degree of poverty which, it is presumed, nobody can well fall into without extreme bad conduct.[69]

The shame of poverty and the need for charity result in interventions being rejected. Therefore, the solution to poverty is increased economic growth and a healthy free market, which will enable those in work to earn a wage to buy necessities. In a society that promotes independence and self-sufficiency, the shame of being unable to meet your own needs, and those of your family, is an emotion that is easily triggered.

Zygmunt Bauman argues that the 'new poor' are those who are unable to consume and participate; the 'flawed consumers'.[70] In our consumer-driven society he argues that it is the inability to spend which in itself creates exclusion, and a sense of being outside the mainstream. If affirmation comes through expenditure, as Bauman argues, then the experience of poverty in a highly consumer-driven society will bring its own degree of shame, again differently from that experienced in other periods.

The story that 'poverty is failure' and, in particular, individual failure, results in a sense of shame. It assumes that others are not equally dependent and not equally vulnerable. If poverty was instead seen as being down to luck – collateral damage in a fast-moving economy – it could make it no more shameful than needing surgery or education.

Finding people who are poor and willing to speak publicly about their position is hard, because the sense of shame is so widespread. The persistence of shame also inhibits the creation of solutions. It makes it difficult to devise innovative and different approaches, in a partnership with people who are themselves poor. Unlike in so many other areas of social policy where the 'user voice' has proven to have such power and impact, the 'shamed voice' of poor people in the relief of poverty is too frequently unheard. But shame can provoke action.

It is commonly said that poverty is a 'shame on our nation', as child poverty is a 'scar on the soul of Britain'. There may be more dominant reasons to tackle poverty, but the shameful fact that poverty exists in a wealthy country such as ours may be one.

Fear

The fear felt by people in poverty is very real, as is the fear many people have that they will become poor, and sitting alongside this is a very evident fear of people who are poor.

People experiencing poverty fear that they will not be able to make ends meet – 37 per cent of non-working adults with children under 16 said not being able to afford food and clothing was their main fear.[71] They fear that they may always struggle or might become poorer. In describing what living on benefits is like, the *Times* columnist Caitlin Moran writes of her childhood:

> Well, mainly, you're scared. You're scared that the benefits will be frozen, or cut, or done away with completely. I don't remember an age where I wasn't scared our benefits would be taken away. It was an anxiety that felt like a physical presence in my chest – a small, black, eyeless insect that hung off my ribs.[72]

People are very afraid of being poor in old age, whether they are already receiving their state pension and struggling or worrying about their future. This is inevitably compounded by the fear that we will be unable to afford the care we need as we are all living longer, or would only be able to pay for it by leaving relatives in poverty.

People who are not poor are also afraid of experiencing poverty. This is unsurprising, given the dynamic nature of poverty and the fluid borderline between poverty and 'getting by'. This fear rapidly and inevitably leads to stories about people in poverty that focus on difference, offering assurance that 'it can never happen to me'.

Describing people in poverty as feckless and bad at budgeting is an easy way of getting some ultimately false comfort that good sense can protect us from this peril.

Fear infects the debate in another powerful way, and that is through a fear of people in poverty. There is an almost timeless sense that people without material wealth should be feared for the damage they can do to the wealthy. There is fear that poor people will take things from the rest, will challenge the status quo and are dangerous because they have so little at stake.

Plato, writing in *The Republic*, said:

> Wealth and poverty: the one is the parent of luxury and indolence, and the other of meanness and viciousness, and both of discontent.[73]

Poverty has been seen as a threat to the established order since the earliest days, especially to people with property. The 'meanness and viciousness' that Plato deplored found their exact parallels in the sixteenth century when displaced unemployed people became described as wanderers, vagrants or vagabonds, striking fear as they wandered about in search of work and shelter. The ruling and middle classes associated these wandering labourers with crime and social disturbance. They were an underclass outside normal social control. They did not fit into the rigid social hierarchy and answered to no master. There were also occasional riots and this exacerbated the fear of revolt.[74]

In nineteenth-century Britain the 'lumpenproletariat, the street folk, the social outcasts, the residuum, and the dangerous classes' were viewed with a mixture of fear, contempt and suspicion.[75] With the deterioration of the labour market in the late 1800s, the Charity Organisation Society feared increasing pauperism and inequality and as such the rise of the 'dangerous classes'. They perceived themselves as the 'resident gentry', checking these tendencies.[76] Even in the twentieth century, welfare measures have been in part a reaction to this fear of the lower classes.[77]

Where housing is cheaper or where the government provides subsidized public housing, or where major industries move out of an area, leaving many residents without jobs, poorer people tend to be grouped together. The problem for those concerned with social order and protection of property comes when poverty is concentrated in particular neighbourhoods and when the opportunities for social mobility, 'the solvent for discontent', are cut off.[78]

Unemployed people are then often portrayed as having criminal or delinquent tendencies and exhibiting weakness of character (often loosely associated with mental illness). These perceived attributes make them a convenient scapegoat. The disturbances and riots in the 1980s in Brixton, Bristol and Liverpool were rapidly associated with concentrations of poverty, despite the fact that many of those involved drew a much closer link with police harassment and a breakdown in confidence in policing.[79]

Fear of crime, violence and other deviancy is readily converted to fear of poor people, and the places where they live. This was evident in many of the responses to the August 2011 riots, which described the rioters as a 'feral underclass ... cut off from the mainstream in everything but its materialism.'[80]

Fear of people in poverty and what they might do if left neglected has itself been a powerful motivator for political and social reforms. The early Poor Law, the welfare changes of the nineteenth century and the founding documents, and later commentary, of the welfare state all recognize the risk posed by poor people.

But fear takes different forms. Fear of revolution and of poor places may prompt action to alleviate poverty but it will also shape the nature of the intervention. State, charitable or corporate interventions springing from a sense of fear will show characteristics of control and rationing. They will be delivered at the individual, or possibly the household level, but they will almost certainly resist attempts to empower the people they support, or give them any independence. At a time when many fear increasing poverty, interventions will also tend to avoid anything that suggests poor people are somehow benefiting from their poverty.

Disgust

The emotion of disgust is, perhaps, a rather surprising one to identify in modern conversations on poverty, but it has been prevalent since the earliest discussions of poverty.

The nineteenth-century social reformers commented on the lifestyle and cleanliness, or otherwise, of those they were trying to save.

Language and narrative of disgust are closely associated with British writing about Irish immigrants in the nineteenth century. The Gordon riots, ostensibly triggered by a fear that Irish immigrants would take the jobs of the indigenous British, were laced with heavy emphasis on the drunkenness, excessive reproduction and general idleness of the newly arrived Irish.

This whole group of people was seen as chaotic, bad with money and with loose morals, which merited disgust and supported political fear of a group taking orders from a foreign power, used to justify laws against Catholics.

An almost identical discourse was then applied to African Americans for most of the twentieth century. They were in turn described in tones of disgust, with a particular emphasis on absent fathers and deserted mothers, slovenliness, dependence on drugs and violence. All of these themes come together in the current UK description of people in poverty, which variously depicts them as bad money managers, idle, obese, tattooed, drug and alcohol dependent and – again – having too many children. The media has done much to create and reinforce feelings of disgust. A particular and more recent elaboration of this emotion of disgust can be seen in how the health, and in particular the weight, of poorer people is described. Ignoring entirely the evidence about the consumption of food high in fat and sugar in poor areas, obesity and associated problems are repeatedly ascribed to poorer people and their families. Modern disgust at poverty is too frequently expressed as disgust at the bodies of those poor people.

The attitude of disgust leads to a belief that change can only come from the individual. The possibility of change is then summarily dismissed, ignoring the very real strength and capability demonstrated by people in poverty. This attitude in turn encourages approaches that punish or curb the behaviour of people in poverty.

The idea of issuing families with an electronic card that will only allow them to spend their benefits on 'essential items' recurs in Parliament and the media. Polling for a Demos report found that over half of respondents felt benefits should not be used to buy cigarettes and alcohol, and other things that are bad for your health. The very real value of population-wide public health initiatives, such as reducing harmful drinking, smoking, drug misuse and improving diet, is distorted yet again into a critique of the lifestyles of people who are poor.

Difference

Running through each of these feelings – shame, fear and disgust – is a strong emphasis on difference. People in poverty feel this difference to a degree, and the perennial demand for politicians to live the life of someone with little money reveals a shared fascination with difference. This is a rather gimmicky attempt – with all the limitations and misleading effects of any short-term project – to encourage wealthier people to acknowledge this distance in hope of generating empathy and potential change.

More significantly, difference emerges within political debate and public opinion. There is a belief that people in poverty make different decisions, are driven by different motives, have different values and behaviours, and lead very different lives from those not in poverty. Although poverty does create a different framework for making basic decisions, and a life in poverty is different from a life of plenty, this is generally because of the framework rather than irrational decisions by people in poverty. The emphasis on difference and the idea of 'them' and 'us' reduces both empathy and public support.

Social distance has made it easier for those considering interventions to imagine how people in poverty think and respond, and to exhibit absolute ignorance about their lives.

Danny Dorling has demonstrated quite how geographically segregated people are on the basis of income and wealth.[81] There is increasingly little prospect of people with very different incomes living side by side, and this geographic distance creates a conceptual and emotional distance that enables poor people to be seen as entirely different. This assumed difference is a striking phenomenon in a world where empathy and understanding is expected, indeed demanded, for all sorts of people, and where understanding and awareness are not based purely on whether you live near someone or not.

The attitude that sees poor people as essentially different results in policy and practice based on a view of poor people as essentially homogeneous, subject to similar impulses and therefore liable to respond to pressure in an identical manner. So attempts to mould behaviour rely on simple interventions, frequently ignoring the complexity of people's lives, the very great range of life experiences, and the vastly different circumstances of people simply described as 'poor'.

Most strikingly, and most damagingly for any notion of progress, it assumes a static quality to the experience of poverty, suggesting that poverty is a long-term identity rather than a situation experienced by large numbers of people for different periods of their lives.

Mistrust

Emotional responses of shame, fear, disgust and difference are enhanced in the current context of a deepening mistrust.

This helps to explain why attitudes towards people in poverty are hardening and support for welfare spending is decreasing. There is mistrust in institutions, neighbourhoods and communities, among elected representatives, doctors, lawyers, bankers and retailers.

We find it increasingly easy to mistrust generally. We are sceptical about the ability of our elected representatives to make decisions about how to help people in poverty, and we are increasingly distrustful of people in poverty, particularly if they seem to be deriving any benefit from their circumstances. So too we are more likely to distrust the institutions created to assist, believing that they can have neither the competence nor the capability of achieving change. Commonly quoted criticisms of social workers and others charged with supporting those in poverty contribute to a narrative that mistrusts any process or intervention, and so casts doubt on the possibility of achieving any sort of outcome.

These feelings of shame, fear, disgust, difference and social distance can be traced through the centuries with more or less emphasis on different aspects at different times.

Our emotional responses to poverty display a feeling of difference between those who are poor and those who are not, as well as feelings of fear and disgust about people in poverty. The striking consistency of these attitudes towards poor people, and the influence on the remedies proposed, suggests that progress will never be made while these attitudes go unacknowledged and unchallenged.

But to leave the discussion of attitudes there would be doing a disservice to those groups who receive particularly hostile reactions – people whose poverty is described in terms of another attribute, such as disability and ill health, motherhood, race and ethnicity. These complex attitudes relate to feelings of difference and do clearly drive public policy and practice interventions.

Disabled people

Both traditional and current attitudes towards disabled people and those with long-term medical conditions are particularly fraught, ranging from patronizing to overtly hostile.

Most religious traditions urge kindness and charity to the 'lame and the halt' and the Victorian literature that shapes so much of our sensibility is particularly sentimental about those who through infirmity are unable to work.

Since then, the impact of activism and demands for equal treatment by disabled people and supporters has created, theoretically at least, a much greater sense of equality.

Campaigns for improved physical access, the closure of large-scale institutional care homes, and the passing of the Disability Discrimination Act 1995 should have altered both the conversation about, and the experience of, disabled people from what was previously condescending and damagingly protective. But the opposite has occurred.

Nine out of ten people with learning difficulties say they have been harassed or bullied in the previous year, and of those who have been frightened or attacked due to their disability, 35 per cent were assaulted, 18 per cent were robbed and 15 per cent spat on.[82]

The press rhetoric about scroungers and layabouts regularly features disabled people. There is a constant and dangerous description of the malingering ill, normally applied to those without visible signs of impairment. Scope reports that 73 per cent of disabled people surveyed had experienced the assumption that they do not work and 46 per cent said people's attitudes towards them have got worse.[83]

It has become all too common to see disabled people as automatically unwilling to work despite more than half of disabled working-age adults being in paid work in 2011. Moreover, 20 per cent of disabled people and those with long-term illnesses who are not working want to (and are able to) work.[84] Many voluntary organizations focus on making employment possible for those who can work, and building confidence in those who feel unable to. Nevertheless, recent research for the RNIB reported that less than one-third of blind people are in work, a figure that has not altered in thirty years.[85]

Those who are unable to work, and particularly those who need additional support, are frequently seen as an unaffordable extra burden on an already stretched budget. As veteran activist and researcher Jenny Morris posted on her blog: 'What's your plan for these people whose lives we apparently can't afford?'[86]

Our current debate has become poisonous, and generations of sympathy have been relatively recently replaced with naked hostility.

These hostile attitudes and increasingly vicious discussion have a direct effect on policy and are used in turn to justify policy. They create a climate of mistrust between disabled people and the state, and between disabled people and non-disabled people, where collusion is suspected between doctor and patient. The emphasis is on the need to prove you are 'disabled enough' not to work through a short Work Capability Test. This process has been widely criticized by disability activists, doctors and their advisers, and is a reaction to our previous inability to engage in an economically productive way.

How did this happen? How did we move from arguing for the right to work, placing expectations on employers to maximize opportunities for disabled people, to giving license for attacks on individuals, and a widespread assumption that disability has been either feigned or exaggerated?

Dame Carol Black, in her important and influential research on the value of work, argues that the exclusion of sick and disabled people from the workforce is damaging to their health and well-being.[87] She urges employers to adopt different attitudes to the employment of people who face obstacles, and identifies the attitudes and behaviours of employers as crucial in improving the health and employability of the workforce. Black did not fully investigate the impact of poor-quality work on health and well-being, but by promoting the social value of work she has drawn attention to how many people – previously deemed incapable of work – have been excluded from the workforce.

These powerful, well-evidenced and valid arguments have provided some of the intellectual ballast for the 'requirement to work' policy, and the use of the benefits system to encourage people to work, regardless of their capability, or the availability of suitable work.

Again we see the role of attitudes in both supporting and driving public policy.

Motherhood

A perennial concern for politicians, the press and policy-makers alike is the issue of mothers who work. Anxiety about the impact of working mothers on the well-being of children is not hard to find. The combination of working mothers, neglected children and poor-quality childcare is a heady brew, regularly blamed for a number of our social ills.

Challenges to better-off mothers who choose to work are common, and there is frequent criticism of working mothers who use nurseries or childcare (with a recent description of nurseries as places to 'park' babies).[88] Media claims that 'working mothers risk damaging their child's prospects' are common.[89]

In sharp contrast, there is an expectation that poorer mothers will need to work if they are to live at anything other than subsistence level. For example, the 2012 US presidential candidate Mitt Romney was reportedly advocating that mothers should go to work 'to have the dignity of work'[90] while in the United Kingdom, childcare policies and rhetoric support mothers who aspire to 'work hard and get on' over those who do not work.[91]

The basis for the argument is clear. Many women have fought and argued for the importance of their engagement in the labour market. Work has brought more than valuable income for many women, and has contributed to their empowerment.

But lying behind the rational argument is an insistence that poorer mothers *must* work, that they must do so when their children are very young, and that the notion of choice is not available to them. This argument is driven by the idea that women earning relatively low wages, feeling forced to work to maintain a standard of living, will resent poorer women, and specifically those receiving benefits, if they are able to spend more time with their children.

There are similar attitudes determined by income, linked to arguments about what choices should be open to mothers who are in poverty. Poor mothers who have a lot of children are seen as morally weak. This is rooted in a deep and recurrent fear that the children of very poor people will become a cost to the current tax payer and a burden on future generations – or at worst a threat to their well-being.

These attitudes have driven policy ideas. Recently, Work and Pensions Secretary Iain Duncan Smith proposed to limit numbers of children for whom child benefit will be paid, because of the cost, because of claims that children's lives are destroyed by workless parents and because children 'need also to learn that it's the right thing for parents to go to work.'[92]

Some headlines expressed outrage at this suggestion while others said 'Stop this hysteria! Why should the state pay for women on benefits to have more than two children?'[93] and 'The 190 families with ten children who cost you more than £11 million in benefits A YEAR'.[94]

It has become possible to vilify mothers on low incomes who stay at home and do not work. This treats the children of poor people as further proof of irresponsible behaviour, not as investments in the future, providing stability and a longer-term stake in society. What is more, it offers a marked contrast to the attitudes expressed about better-off mothers who also work.

Race and ethnicity

Attitudes and feelings of hostility towards particular groups because of a perceived heightened social distance are often linked to fear. These attitudes towards black and minority ethnic (BME) people in poverty are particularly hostile and homogenizing.

Research funded by the JRF shows that poverty is higher among BME groups than the white population but also demonstrates that there are significant differences within BME groups. For example, Bangladeshis have the lowest inequality between incomes but the highest poverty rate, whereas Indian people have high income inequality and above-average poverty rates. There are differences between Hindus, who are more advantaged, and Muslims, who are less so. There are also differences within these groups, for example, depending on household size and structure.[95]

There are vast differences within the United Kingdom's BME population and the relationship between different issues such as identity, religion, gender, family, culture, location, disability, employment, education and so on makes it very difficult to describe the 'group's' experience of poverty.[95] Different groups face varying barriers in accessing work, education and public services. Individuals within and between groups have varying caring responsibilities that can affect their ability to work and join different social networks that could provide access to jobs.

In-work poverty can be affected by workplace culture such as training and progression opportunities. As such, solutions would also be different for different groups. For example, research comparing experiences of poverty in Bradford found that Bangladeshi people needed more opportunities to diversify beyond low-paid work (predominantly in restaurants), whereas African Caribbean men particularly needed skills to access full-time employment.[96]

There are also hostile attitudes towards white people living in poverty. Harris Beider's work has challenged the stereotypes of white working-class neighbourhoods where poverty is perceived as inevitable, and unemployment, stupidity and extremist views are imagined to be common.[97] The reality shows a complex array of feelings from residents who felt they were looked down on and that they were 'last in line', neglected by local and national politicians.

Despite these marked and important differences, generalizations about the experience of black people in poverty are common, and frequently demonstrate a very particular degree of hostility.

Local blight

There have always been poor places and we have always been concerned about them, because of cost, waste and risk as well as feelings of shame and fear.

Across the United Kingdom there were places of transit with concentrations of poor people, such as London's East End, which was famously home to French Huguenots, Russian exiles, European Jews and more recently Bengali families. While offering sanctuary, they also generated solidarity and support, and most importantly routes out, so that successive waves of migrants spent time in the East End and moved onwards as their own economic circumstances improved.

The rapid pace of industrialization, and the consequent development of slum dwellings, led to great anxiety across the United Kingdom about both the physical and moral degradation of slum living. Mass slum clearance was a major policy response, but it had its precursors in waves of social reformers expressing the very same combination of fear and disgust that seem to have characterized attitudes to concentrations of poverty.

These concerns were mirrored almost exactly by anxiety about 'those inner cities', as Margaret Thatcher termed them in 1987. Riots took place in 1981 in Brixton, Birmingham, Leeds and Liverpool and again in 1985 in Birmingham, and tensions were heightened with the creation of a 'stop and search' policy.

The same fearful unfocused anxiety is readily expressed about former industrialized areas, such as Hartlepool, Sunderland and Merthyr Tydfil, where it is frequently asserted that not enough has been done to provide alternative employment opportunities and to support communities.

A shared thread of emotional response runs through all of these concerns. This manifests itself in a view that these areas are ungovernable, and that they are so entirely different from other parts of the county that only a very major intervention could ever work. This in turn allows the policy maker to see the problems as simply too vast for intervention.

These concerns over 'poor people living in poor areas' – sometimes, although not always, linked to ethnicity – have re-emerged in response to the 2011 riots. There is an additional focus on outer estates, where many of the same issues have emerged as in inner-city council estates, where people are not transient and can feel trapped. Policies emerged around 'regeneration and renewal' and 'community cohesion'.

Attitudes of fear, disgust and shame at living in certain places can be readily identified. But most strikingly so is the notion that these places are entirely different, with a sense of culpability for those who live there. These views are reinforced by the stories we tell ourselves; that nothing can be done about these places and that they are doomed to failure.

These attitudes reveal a simplified understanding of areas. Far from being 'broken' communities that are condemned to poverty, social problems and lawlessness, many of these are disadvantaged but also resilient communities that are capable of surviving shock events and can adapt and change.

There are countless community projects that engage people in deprived areas and build their skills and confidence. These include Dads' Gardening Project in Templehall (Kirkcaldy), which aimed to help isolated young fathers,[98] and the Gellideg Foundation, formed by mothers who wanted to improve their community and provide childcare.

These initiatives now manage projects that include activities with older people, job training and managing community buildings, providing people with confidence through volunteering and activities for those in the community.[99]

Community networks are strong in many places. A JRF report looking at six deprived neighbourhoods revealed that, in most, residents emphasized the strength and tenacity of family and social networks in their local area. Although neighbourly ties were more variable, 'there was little evidence from the interviews with residents to support current political rhetoric about "broken" communities or "broken" families'.[100]

And there are occasions of more informal types of mutual support. One resident from West Marsh, Grimsby, spoke about a local system of shared childcare to enable other mothers to attend the job centre.[100]

Serious attempts at a strategy for cities can be hampered by policy makers ignoring the complexities and positive aspects of specific places. There are ways of practically improving areas, but to do so means focusing on the right issues.

Anne Power's *Phoenix Cities* explores the regeneration that took place in cities in Europe and the United States.[101] The cities in this study focused on providing for people who already lived in them, through strategies for physical and environmental restoration, economic development and social reinvestment. This was supported by state leaders in the United States and civic leaders in Europe being able to transform places thanks to a clear vision of what they could become. There is tremendous unease about doing this in the United Kingdom, where there is a great emphasis on attracting different people to a place, rather than providing for the people who already live there.

Our attitudes towards particular places are driven by our emotions, particularly of fear and difference, which in a context of mistrust further reduces public support for solving poverty.

Welfare

As noted earlier, support for welfare spending (Figure 3.1) has significantly decreased, particularly among 18–24-year-olds, where the proportion fell from around 50 per cent in 1987 to 20 per cent in 2011.[102]

The perceived link between benefits and dependency is also evident: 2012 YouGov research revealed that 69 per cent of people agreed with the view that

Britain's current welfare system has created a culture of dependency, whereby many people, and often whole families, get used to living off state benefits; the system needs to be radically changed to get such people to take more responsibility for their lives and their families.

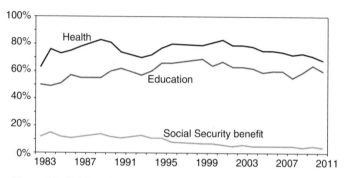

Figure 3.1. Public attitudes: first or second priorities for extra government spending. *Source*: British Social Attitudes Survey, NatCen.

This is compared with 22 per cent who felt that 'most people who rely on welfare benefits are victims of circumstances beyond their control [and that] the benefits they receive are far from generous, and are the least a civilised society should provide in order to help them and their families avoid abject poverty'.[103]

Poverty, welfare, 'idleness' and reliance are bound together in conceptual confusion. 'Idleness' is not evident among the majority of people in poverty, nor is it by any means restricted to them. There are wealthy people with no requirement to work for a living. Although there is a growing disgust about wealthy people who pay themselves large sums of money, this is much less marked than disgust about people in poverty who do not work. It seems that it is perfectly acceptable to be unemployed if the material conditions are good enough. So reliance on others is not in itself a bad thing. Inherited wealth is not uncommon and is widely accepted. Indeed popular culture often celebrates those made wealthy through fortune or family, e.g. *Heir Hunters* and *Hello* magazine. Why is it that we can tolerate the wealthy person who is dependent, but feel contempt towards a dependent person in poverty?

The distaste is specifically targeted at people who rely on welfare benefits. The surprising thing here is that all of us are enormously dependent upon state provision for our health care, education, national security, roads, transport and police. The receipt of universal services, used regardless of income, attracts little stigma. There is far less hostility towards those receiving tax credits, which are claimed by 54 per cent of couples with children, 10 per cent of single people and 80 per cent single parents.[104] The total expenditure of tax credits is nearly £30 billion, with over 6 million families receiving some form of tax credit.[105]

Even though social security, such as Jobseeker's Allowance, is also a universally accessible service, this attracts much more audible hostility. Political and public disdain is reserved for those who are perceived to be 'overly reliant' on the state. There is a perception that 'over reliance' creates dependency. As mentioned earlier, in 2011, 54 per cent felt that if benefits were lower people would learn to stand on their own two feet.[106] This contempt is also linked to 'idleness'.

Just as the United Kingdom has its 'skivers vs strivers' or 'shirkers vs workers' debate, American debate pits 'moochers' – those who take and sponge off others while doing nothing for themselves – against the hard-working creators.

These distinctions create tension between those who are working hard, and behaving properly, the 'deserving poor', and those who lead a life of apparent luxury on benefits,

whose misfortunes can all be found in their individual character – the 'undeserving'.

There is no intrinsic problem with descriptions of this sort.
Typologies are, after all, the stuff of social policy. But these
distinctions are both meaningless and damaging.

They are meaningless because as all the evidence demonstrates, people who are struggling to get by on a very low income with no personal assets are far more likely to become
unemployed, and get described as 'idle' in another carelessly
used description. In short, today's shirker could be yester-
day's worker.

These distinctions are also damaging because they dis-
tort the direction of public policy. They make the organizing
purpose of policy the attempt to shift people into work, or
in other ways penalize those without work, without understanding the fluid nature of these categories, and the complexity masked by careless labels.

It is unclear whether people disapprove of dependency
as a personal attribute, or whether hostility comes from the
cost, or perceived cost, to the taxpayer. It is almost certainly a
combination of the two.

It has become common to describe the population as if it
is divided into two: the taxpayer earning money, and paying
it to the benefit claimant, who is earning nothing. All the evidence contradicts this easy picture, but it undoubtedly has
considerable impact. It is a familiar way of describing the current contract and directly feeds the notion that taxpayers and
claimants are different groups of people.

Our rhetoric is also concerned with dependency and over
reliance because of its association with 'cheats'. There is a
growing anger about inequality and about people who are,
or are perceived to be, cheating the system. This is reflected
in some views about the very wealthy who avoid tax, for

example, but political debate and the media give most attention to the 'cheats' who receive benefits.

The idea of fairness or 'pulling one's weight' is related to this. Polls have frequently shown that the public fear unfairness most of all.

In Policy Exchange research, 63 per cent defined fairness as 'getting what you deserve' or 'reciprocity' or 'something for something', as opposed to 26 per cent who associated fairness with equality.[107] This reveals strong support for policies that advocate people should do more to earn their benefits, as well as benefit sanctions.[108]

The tabloids highlight stories about those on benefits who live in 'mansions' paid for by the taxpayer. Some get 'handouts' and choose not to work, while others struggle and work 'every hour God sends'.

The government continues to use language and ideas of 'fairness' to justify policies, as George Osborne's rhetoric demonstrates: 'Where is the fairness, we ask, for the shift worker, leaving home in the dark hours of the early morning, who looks up at the closed blinds of their next door neighbour sleeping off a life on benefits?'[109]

However, just like dependency, people rarely look at fairness and inequality from the perspective of the person in poverty. It is undoubtedly unfair that some people have long-term medical conditions that make it impossible for them to

> As part of Poverty Alliance's Evidence Participation and Change project, research was carried out by lone parents involved with Fife Gingerbread to explore the experiences of lone parents living on low incomes in a rural community. One respondent says:
>
> 'I am sort of isolating myself from my family as I don't like them to see that [my child's] very poor, you know I wouldn't invite my friends over either.'

take on paid work. It is unfair that in some parts of the country the prospects of getting stable, long-term paid work are vanishingly small. It is equally unfair that rents are much higher in some parts of the country than others. And it is unfair that the life prospects of children born to wealthy families are so very much greater than those of children born in poverty. So much is true.

So how, then, could public attitudes to poverty start to shift? We could think entirely differently about welfare and poverty. Stephen Crossley, of North East Child Poverty, recommends using the public's strong belief that poverty is caused by individual behaviour to challenge the language we use.

> Save the Children and others provide platforms for people to speak about their experiences. *Taking a Closer Look: Child Poverty and Disability Northern Ireland* describes a number of families' experiences, such as Jill and James, who have two children, one of whom has physical and learning disabilities and needs constant supervision. Both parents work part time but find the higher costs associated with having a disabled child financially difficult.

He suggests we should look at the 'cycle of privilege', as opposed to poverty, at 'intergenerational advantage' instead of intergenerational unemployment, and 'tax evasion/avoidance as a lifestyle choice', as opposed to benefits.[110] This challenge to language associated with poverty, welfare, 'idleness' and dependency creates more objective discussions about poverty and its solutions, where we can examine not just the welfare system but wider factors.

We will have to change the framework of the debate if we are to develop effective solutions and attract greater public support, but, as I have argued here, emotions get in the way.

Chapter 4

Is poverty inevitable?

The emotional and conceptual factors that prevent us from tackling poverty are related to the belief that poverty is inevitable. In part, this can be seen when people use the New Testament quote out of its original context, shrug their shoulders and say, 'well, the poor will always be with us'.

On top of that there is a seductive consensus that sees poverty as inevitable because it is an intrinsic by-product of our competitive age. NatCen's research found that 35 per cent of people thought that poverty was 'an inevitable part of modern life' (Figure 4.1). This proportion has remained more or less constant since 1986.[111]

This acceptance is shared across party political lines but results in two different arguments; poverty is entirely created by the political and economic institutions and structure of society; or poverty is a matter of individual capability, character and innate weakness.

Those who believe that poverty is caused by the structure of our economic system argue that we can only tackle deep-seated poverty by overthrowing that system, while their opponents argue for wholesale change in individuals and communities.

Neither position is wholly right, and, by oversimplifying the causes of poverty, our efforts to tackle it are destined to be ineffective. Poverty is not inevitable.

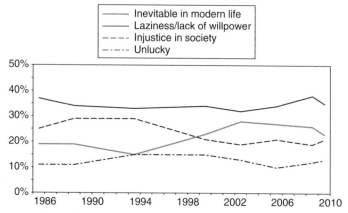

Figure 4.1. Public attitudes to the causes of people living in need. *Source*: British Social Attitudes Survey, NatCen.

There are structural causes for poverty, just as there are individual routes into (and out of) poverty. The danger is that the logic of both positions can lead to an acceptance that poverty is a 'natural' consequence of our society and economy and that it is impossible to imagine alternatives. They raise such a high barrier to achieving change that it is all too easy for the casual bystander to turn away and shrug their shoulders; the problem is simply too big. The competing views cancel each other out and nothing changes. So the first step is to chip away at the barriers created by these beliefs.

> Poverty is not natural. It is man-made and it can be overcome and eradicated by the actions of human beings.
>
> — *Nelson Mandela*

Changing public beliefs about poverty

Social change happens imperceptibly, though not necessarily slowly. It has many parents and the path to achieving it is never linear. The following components can be identified in most social change movements:

- a crisis/culmination of beliefs that demands something must be done and provides motive;
- agitation – an expression of anger, hostility and what is often described as extreme responses;
- an alliance of people arguing for change – the strongest alliances bring together people with different perspectives and motives;
- a shared idea of both the problem and the solution;
- a tested solution.

Social change has usually been driven by those who experience disadvantage or inequality. The liberation movements of the 1960s and 70s gave loud and angry voice to women fighting for equality, to gay men and lesbians, to black and minority ethnic people, and to disabled people.

These movements were built around a set of grievances, challenging demands and a prescribed answer to the problem.

Women's fight for the vote was born of the belief that women should have the same democratic rights as men. Anger and hostility emerged and action often took the form of 'extreme responses' from particular groups. There was a shared narrative and solution, but not always a shared method (the Suffragettes and Suffragists, for example, disagreed over election policy).

> JRF and the *Guardian*'s Breadline Britain series gave people the chance to describe the reality of living in poverty and their own experiences, such as a single mother in Leeds who described the struggle of providing for her two children and wanting to develop her own skills as well.[1]

Some saw votes for women as a step towards further equality while others never envisaged women entering parliament. Some saw it as a reward for their contribution to the war effort and others perceived suffrage as part of a wider trend towards democratic equality. Similar debates emerged over equal pay for women, which, although it had been an issue decades before, became critical in 1968 when female Ford Dagenham workers were re-graded unfairly and went on strike. As with all social change, powerful advocates and allies, in this case the trade unions and Labour Party, played their part.

Why has there rarely been any similar movement of people in poverty in the United Kingdom? It is partly because of the very changeable nature of poverty. Many people experience poverty at different times of their lives – some research suggests that around half of the UK population will experience at least one year in relative income poverty[112] at some point, so it is not surprising that people do not identify themselves in this way.

Very transient conditions may be damaging and unpleasant, but they are unlikely to generate great movements of protest. There may be a definable population of people in poverty at any point in time but people in poverty are not a static group. It is a state that many people move in and out of for varying periods of time, except for those in deep, persistent poverty.

There are two other factors that, in an even more profound way, inhibit a protest movement of people in poverty. First, as we have seen, there is a deep and enduring sense of shame about poverty, and this pervasive emotion makes it hard for people to speak up. And second, the lack of material resources that is characteristic of poverty makes self-organization more difficult.

Advocacy organizations have been readily dismissed by opponents as woolly minded, politically motivated or having other vested interests, and it is striking how rarely churches, trade unions and voluntary organizations, which might have been expected to line up with those experiencing poverty, offer them a platform.

The experience of poverty itself has not, until recently, been the subject of advocacy by those who are themselves affected, and it has therefore always risked losing the authenticity, and the passion, of other campaigns.

However, a great deal has changed in the last few years. In part this has been the result of welfare reform's impact and the tide of protest and anxiety unleashed by opponents of those welfare changes. But undoubtedly change has been enhanced by social media, which provides a platform that people experiencing poverty can use. This platform can be anonymous, if desired, and is generally cheaper and more convenient than self-organization and promotion, which is often prohibitively expensive. People in poverty are increasingly speaking out about their experiences despite negative attitudes from the public and the media.

Many are directly challenging the idea that they are 'skivers, shirkers or victims'. A number of inspired, and inspiring, bloggers have used social media to challenge the dominant discourse and voice their experience of a life in poverty.

In her blog *A Girl Called Jack*,[113] Jack Monroe vividly describes life without work and without money, while Kaliya Franklin, in her blog *Benefit Scrounging Scum*,[114] has provided a powerful insight into the lives of people with disabilities. Along with Sue Marsh's *Diary of a Benefit Scrounger*,[115] they provide a platform for people who are otherwise voiceless in this debate. They express thoughts about the experience of poverty as well as solutions.

The recent 'We Are Spartacus' *Report on the Proposed Changes to Disability Living Allowance: Diary of a Benefit Scrounger* received significant social media attention. It was researched, written and supported by disabled people and aimed to challenge the language of the dominant debate as well as the policies:

> We have been subjected to poor reforms, ever tougher sanctions, and an insidious, scrounger rhetoric from both politicians and the press. Our input and opinions have all too often been ignored... This report aims to give a voice to the millions of sick and disabled people who rely on effective support to live productive lives. It aims to present a strong evidence base on which to build effective reform.[116]

Social media also facilitated the existence of UK Uncut, which sprang out of the Twitter hashtag #ukuncut. It demonstrates the power of both social media and protest in giving voice to people who advocate for an alternative – that the government can make savings without policies that target the poorest people in society. It currently focuses on tax evasion and clear links are being made between 'tax dodgers' and 'austerity cuts'.

The voices of those affected are not, however, the only ingredients in social change. The identification of a crisis is also part of such change. Two distinct and different crises are identified in the context of poverty.

There is a poverty lobby that sees a crisis in people living below a socially sustainable level – people who are compelled by an uncaring bureaucracy to jump through hoops to get even the small amount of benefits provided by a grudging state, effectively casting them adrift in a greedy world that provides insufficient support. This view has its angry advocates, many of them people personally affected, and behind it is a broad alliance of different organizations offering support. It has motive too, as its supporters believe the state is the best organizer of a response to the problem.

The 'poverty lobby' is not the only group that sees a crisis. There are others who are concerned about the high levels of state subsidy and believe the welfare bill at a time of austerity has reached crisis levels. These advocates make an unarguable and strong moral case about the impact of reliance on the state by some elements of society. This argument has also led to considerable agitation, based on the belief that the intervention of the state itself is sapping human potential. A strong alliance has built up between those who tell a compelling story of wasted lives and a trapped underclass. There is motive here too, about reducing the role of the state, and its power to influence lives, as well as wishing to reduce the burden of public expenditure.

And there are others. There are strong advocates for community-based responses, arguing for a simpler way of living, a local sharing of common goods, and an end to high consumption as the only satisfactory way of life. There are those who look to the market to respond, believing that caring corporations could hold the solution, giving priority to the well-being of their employees and customers.

In all these arguments there are elements of a movement for change. Between them, there is a general acceptance that there is a crisis that needs urgent action. They all agree that it would be desirable to minimize dependence on welfare and that employment is better than unemployment for most people.

But at this point, opinions become divided and there is no shared belief about the causes of poverty and absolutely no shared solution. The current debate on poverty is shaped by ideological beliefs, which diminish the opportunities for shared endeavour.

It is striking how rarely the prescriptions for poverty (outlined below) are based on evidence, even when poverty is accepted as a phenomenon that exists and is important, as well as one that can be tackled. Instead, they are precisely aligned with the attitudes of the advocate.

A *social administration response* prescribes welfare levels, and debates how different forms of social security influence behaviour. Its advocates recognize the need for a minimum income that an individual cannot fall below, but frequently focus on the relationship between the levels of benefit, how it is provided and the outcomes for individuals and their family.

A *labour market approach* focuses on how the economy, both local and national, generates employment, how this is distributed and how many appropriate jobs there are.

A *regional development/economic response* focuses on the opportunity to generate paid work, particularly in disadvantaged areas, working with the private sector, voluntary organizations and local and regional bodies to create work, and enable people to get into it.

Community-based approaches focus on the need to provide support, but may be more accepting of a world without work, and more interested in the quality of life for people who cannot work, or for whom work is not available. This perspective focuses much more on retaining talent and energy within communities, to generate networks of support, and mutual engagement.

An *individualist response* is concerned with motivation, engaging with individuals, and the power of coaching to enable people to take up opportunities, expand their skills and become 'job ready'. This approach also focuses closely on individual behaviour, and is particularly interested in the characteristics that may make a person poor.

These different perspectives spring from deeply held views about the way the world is and should be organized. They are influenced by the emotions and feelings that this essay has described. They directly shape responses to poverty, and frequently operate in entirely different worlds. Because of this, they continue to hamper our ability to tackle poverty.

However, there have been times when shared responses have made a positive impact on poverty. Efforts in the United States have parallels with what has been attempted in the United Kingdom.

In his 1964 State of the Union address, President Johnson declared an 'unconditional war on poverty in America' to reduce the cost and the waste it imposed. He set a national challenge that would need a number of different strategies to work at state and local level.

The programme included significant infrastructure investment in public housing, roads and public transportation. It increased the minimum wage and extended it to cover nearly all workers, and launched Head Start, Job Corps and a host of other initiatives at State level to improve education. It addressed poverty through a combination of investment, regulation and capacity building (sustainable development that enhances potential).

> We fought a war on poverty and poverty won.
> — *Ronald Reagan*

Many have described this 'war' as a failure and dismissed it as another example of how attempts to intervene in the free market are doomed to disaster. Indeed, trends in official poverty figures have led some to agree with Ronald Reagan that America lost the war on poverty – that the wide range of income support programmes, from food stamps to unemployment insurance, have been ineffective anti-poverty tools.

But it is worth having another look at the impact and reach of these programmes. It is easy to attribute the relative success of the war on poverty to a growing economy in which poverty might have reduced anyway. However, for the period of the 'war', numbers steadily fell (from 19 per cent in 1964 to 12 per cent in 1972), and have rocketed ever since (20 per cent of all American children in poverty and a staggering 40 per cent of African American children).[117]

Important research from Bruce D. Meyer and James X. Sullivan in *Winning the War: Poverty from the Great Society to the Great Recession* reveals even greater success. By using the consumption-based measure – as opposed to the traditional income-based measure, and so accounting for bias in the cost-of-living adjustment – they found that the poverty rate declined by more than 25 percentage points between 1960 and 2010.[118]

There are several explanations for Meyer and Sullivan's findings. Poverty has been sharply reduced in the United States through tax rate cuts, tax credits and increases in social security, but other transfers have played only a small role. It could be that restructuring the economy would have reduced the numbers of people in poverty anyway, or that rising educational attainment could account for some of the decline.

Despite repeated claims of a failure to tackle poverty and focus on the limitations of success, better measures of poverty show a sharp improvement in recent decades, and that targeted economic policies and policies that support growth have had a significant impact. Although improvements have not been as significant compared with prior decades, the noticeable improvements in the last decade are comparable with or better than the progress in the 1980s.

I have described this experiment at some length because of the clear historical and political links with the previous Labour government's project on reducing poverty launched in 1997.

Programmes throughout the period of the administration included the creation of Sure Start, the New Deal for Lone Parents, Tax Credits, the National Minimum Wage, spending on education and the work of the Social Exclusion unit. In addition, Tony Blair announced in March 1999 that child poverty would be abolished within a generation.

Much of the rhetoric and practice in the United Kingdom echoes that of the war on poverty in the United States. The UK version of the war on poverty features the same mixture of capacity building, changes to practice, regulation and a focus on cash transfers. However, this programme also has limitations as well as successes.

Overall, relative poverty fell significantly under the previous Labour government. In Labour's first two terms it fell by 2.4 percentage points (before housing costs (BHC)).[119] Improvements in pensioner and child poverty played a large part in this and were due to substantial spending on benefits and tax credit.

Increases in employment also help to account for the falling proportion of children in workless households.[120] Child poverty (BHC) fell overall between 1997 and 2010, from 26.7 per cent to 18 per cent (Figure 4.2).[121] Children living with lone parents who work part time made the most significant gains as poverty fell by at least 25 per cent (both BHC and AHC).[122] The impact of other initiatives such as Minimum Wage, Sure Start, financial support for childcare and increases in education spending will most likely be long term rather than immediate, and are difficult to evaluate separately to other factors that affect income distribution.[123]

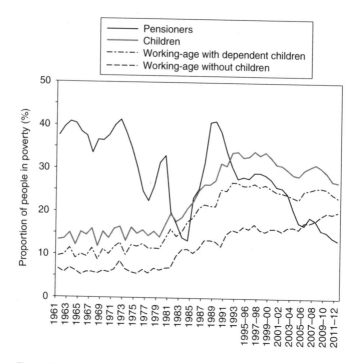

Figure 4.2. Long-term view of poverty. *Source*: Analysis of Family Resources Survey, Institute for Fiscal Studies/Department for Work and Pensions (figures are for Great Britain up to 2001–02 and for the United Kingdom thereafter).

The limitations of the previous Labour government's approach are evident in the fact that there was little improvement for working-age adults without children; a group that has continued to be neglected in efforts to tackle poverty.

There has also been criticism of the expense of interventions. Between 1997–98 and 2010–11 there was an £18 billion annual increase in spending on benefits for families with children and £11 billion on benefits for pensioners.[123] Some argue that reductions in poverty were because of a combination of targeted efforts in good economic times and a general trend towards reductions in poverty.

There was little outward public support for the policies. There was a low public awareness of the child poverty target, and redistribution policies such as benefits and tax credits were rarely boasted about. Research has shown that public attitudes towards redistribution are unfavourable and have been declining since the mid 1990s.[124]

Although relative poverty (BHC) has continued to fall, this was not the case for absolute poverty and material deprivation, where improvements were negligible or poverty rates increased as in 2004–5 to 2007–8, and for some groups in 2009–10 to 2010–11. The absolute living standards of poorer households did not increase – instead standards for households at the bottom of the income distribution fell less than for those in the middle distribution.[125]

Poverty continues in the United Kingdom, as it does in the United States. The Institute for Fiscal Studies predicts that child poverty in the United Kingdom will rise to 24.4 per cent by 2020 (from 19.7 per cent in 2009) and absolute child poverty will increase to 23.1 per cent (from 17 per cent in 2009). This is compared with targets of 10 per cent and 5 per cent respectively. Working-age adults in poverty would increase from 5.7 million in 2009–10 to 7.5 million by 2020–21.[126] Both increases are partly due to the estimated negative impacts of changes to tax and benefit policies.

Chapter 5

Conclusion: how can
we fight poverty?

I t is possible to reduce poverty, but it demands a concerted
and almost certainly expensive effort. Above all, it needs
consistency and a sustained and long-term drive. Work to reduce poverty is frequently unpopular, always contested and
the gains will be slow. Strong alliances, shared motive and
long-term commitment will be necessary.

We will never make that commitment to the long-term,
sustained and costly work that is needed to end poverty if
public support is lacking, incredulous or simply uncommit-
ted. For this, we would need a shared agreement that poverty is too costly, too wasteful and too risky for society. An
agreement about this could ensure that policies to tackle
poverty could stop being seen as an optional extra. It would
instead become a central part of the mission of any government, local and national. It would be a priority for business,
recognizing that a strong economy will never grow without people who can both produce and consume. A shared
response to poverty would galvanize others who have an
interest in a strong and settled economy, and more secure
communities. It would provide an organizing purpose for
the many agencies and charities that currently struggle to

respond to the needs of people and places in poverty. What is more, the communities that so frequently face the appalling effects of deep and persistent poverty would gain confidence from this.

At the centre of this shared acceptance would be a new and more focused social contract that recognizes that neither the state alone, nor the untrammelled market, nor the efforts of individuals can solve poverty alone.

Individuals obviously play a major role in ending their poverty, and can go to extraordinary efforts to improve their own life chances. The market has a role too, as many employers are showing, and the state, both local and national, has an organizing, planning and distributive role. To assume that any of these can end poverty alone is short sighted and doomed to failure. None of this will happen while we use language that describes people in poverty as somehow lacking and entirely different in their behaviours, decisions and aspirations. It will not be possible while we ignore the impacts of poverty, blaming those without money for the circumstances that caused their poverty. But mostly it will not be possible if we persist in thinking of 'the poor' as a fixed category without recognizing the very fluid nature of poverty, and the range of life events that contribute to poverty. We need a new agreement that recognizes a shared interest in reducing poverty and a more rational discussion about the sort of society we want and the routes into and out of poverty.

Work is undoubtedly a route out of poverty for many, but work that offers progression and consistency, and provides enough for people to live decent lives, is not currently available. The Living Wage is a step towards this.

The labour market, as it currently operates, will always need a big state subsidy through tax and benefits to provide in-work support to prevent people from falling into destitution.

A more balanced market, offering more security, could reduce that demand on the state.

A volatile housing market, fuelled by shortage, will result in unaffordable rents – this too will demand a greater call on the scarce resources of the state. A state that manages to accommodate these pivotal markets – through regulation and investment – could then also organize its cash transfers, its social security payments, in a way that meets the needs of people within these markets.

In any complex and fast-moving economy there will be times of greater dependence and times of lesser dependence. There are crisis points in all our lives. There is plenty of advice about clever and cost-effective ways of structuring payments when we are moving into and out of work, not least from the many people who have themselves relied upon the benefit system.

The costs of being poor are great. The cost of finance, utilities and food can all be greater for those with very little, and these costs further trap people whose incomes are in any case low.

None of these aspects are so difficult or overwhelming that they cannot be changed.

There is a counsel of despair that argues that unless we overturn all the institutions of society, we will see no progress for people who are poor. Equally there is a strong view that unless the lives of individuals are transformed by their own graft there will be no end to poverty. Both these views allow wasteful and risky poverty to persist in this relatively wealthy country.

In this book I have sought to demonstrate that poverty continues to matter because of cost, waste and risk, to individuals and to society – the same issues identified by Seebohm Rowntree more than 100 years ago:

No view of the ultimate scheme of things would now be accepted under which multitudes of men and women are doomed by inevitable law to a struggle for existence so severe as necessarily to cripple or destroy the higher parts of their nature.

Our attitudes and stories reflect the lack of public support and are explained by our emotional responses of shame, fear, disgust, difference and mistrust, in addition to our conceptual understanding of poverty and welfare.

Our tendency to focus primarily on individual agency or structural overhaul has further hindered our ability to solve poverty. The stalemate between these arguments has added to a belief that poverty is inevitable.

Emotions get in the way of public support for poverty reduction:

- shame – experienced by people in poverty and reinforced by those who are not;
- fear – of poverty and its effects, strengthened by the stories we tell and attitudes we hold;
- disgust – at the experience of poverty, and especially the assumed behaviour of people who are poor;
- difference – a social distance and difference from people in poverty;
- hostility – towards people in poverty, made more complex and intense for particular groups of people and places.

These emotions compound one another to prohibit effective political leadership, undermine administrative response and strangle effective advocacy.

History shows us that as a society we can have an impact on poverty – it is not impossible.

> Overcoming poverty is not a task of charity, it is an act of justice. Like Slavery and Apartheid, poverty is not natural. It is man-made and it can be overcome and eradicated by the actions of human beings.
>
> — *Nelson Mandela*

Why fight poverty? Because we can fight it and win. By refusing to do so we are entrenching disadvantage in our fractured society and doing it in a way that will cost future generations dear. If our own deep fear of vulnerability leads us to make sweeping judgements about those facing the greatest risks, we fail to take the opportunity to secure lasting social change.

In so doing we avoid the greatest challenge facing social policy in the twenty-first century, which is to maximize the skills and contributions of all our citizens.

Photograph by Liz Hingley.

Endnotes

1. D. Hirsch. 2006. *What Will It Take to End Child Poverty?* Joseph Rowntree Foundation.

2. I. Mulheirn. 2013. The truth about welfare (www.newstatesman .com/politics/politics/2013/05/truth-about-welfare – accessed 9 July 2013). See also J. Griggs and M. Evans. 2010. *A Review of Benefit Sanctions.* Joseph Rowntree Foundation.

3. J. Browne and A. Hood. 2012. *A Survey of the UK Benefit System*, p. 5. Institute for Fiscal Studies.

4. A. Tarr and D. Finn. 2012. *Implementing Universal Credit: Will the Reforms Improve the Service for Users?* Joseph Rowntree Foundation.

5. P. Butler. 2013. Data of how much a typical family will lose in a week: every welfare cut listed. *The Guardian*, 1 April (www.guar dian.co.uk/news/datablog/2013/apr/01/every-welfare-cut-listed – accessed 9 July 2013).

6. H. Aldridge, P. Kenway, T. MacInnes and A. Parkeh. 2012. *Monitoring Poverty and Social Exclusion.* Joseph Rowntree Foundation.

7. C. Goulden. 2010. *Cycles of Poverty, Unemployment and Low Pay*, p. 7. Joseph Rowntree Foundation.

8. N. Meager and E. Carta. 2011. *Skills for Self-Employment: Annex Labour Force Survey analysis, August 2011.* UKCES.

9. M. Goos and A. Manning. 2007. Lousy jobs and lovely jobs: the rising polarization of work in Britain. *The Review of Economics and Statistics* 89(1):118–133.

10. M. Brynin. 2012. *Individual Choice and Risk: The Case of Higher Education.* Institute for Social and Economic Research.

11. K. Skrivankova. 2010. *Between Decent Work and Forced Labour: Examining the Continuum of Exploitation.* Joseph Rowntree Foundation.

12. B. Tunstall, M. Bevan, J. Bradshaw, K. Croucher, S. Duffy, C. Hunter, A. Jones, J. Rugg, A. Wallace and S. Wilcox. 2013. *The Links between Housing and Poverty: An Evidence Review*, p. 5. Joseph Rowntree Foundation.

13. Shelter. The affordability of private renting – small families claiming local housing allowance, p. 5.

14. LSL Property Services plc. 2013. Buy-to-let index.

15. D. Hirsch. 2013. *A Minimum Income Standard for the UK in 2013*. Joseph Rowntree Foundation.

16. Tullett Prebon Strategy Notes. 2013. *Measuring the Real Cost of Living* (Issue 43, 20 February 2013). Tullett Prebon Group Ltd, London.

17. E. Clery, L. Lee and S. Kunz. 2013. *Public Attitudes to Poverty and Welfare, 1983–2011: Analysis Using British Social Attitudes Data*, pp. 16, 23. National Centre for Social Research.

18. Ibid. p. 13.

19. Ibid. p. 23.

20. Ibid. p. 8.

21. C. W. Mills. 1963, 1967. Poverty, craftsmanship, and private troubles and public issues. In *Power, Politics and People. The Collected Essays of C. Wright Mills* (ed. I. H. Horowitz). New York: Oxford University Press.

22. Op. cit., Clery et al. (2013), p. 41.

23. H. Glennerster, J. Hills, D. Piachaud and J. Webb. 2004. *One Hundred Years of Poverty and Policy*, p. 49, Table 2. Joseph Rowntree Foundation.

24. E. Wallis (ed.). 2009. *From the Workhouse to Welfare: What Beatrice Webb's 1909 Minority Report Can Teach Us Today*, p. 16. Fabian Society.

25. J. Harris. 1997. *William Beveridge: A Biography*, p. 482. Oxford University Press.

26. Ibid., p. 146.

27. W. Beveridge. *Voluntary Action*, see Harris (1997), p. 266.

28. C. Carter-Wall and G. Whitfield. 2012. *The Role of Aspirations, Attitudes and Behaviour in Closing the Educational Attainment Gap*, p. 3. Joseph Rowntree Foundation.

29. ONS statistics released 28 November 2012. Underemployment up 1 million since 2008 (www.ons.gov.uk/ons/rel/lmac/underemploy ed-workers-in-the-uk/2012/sty-underemployed-workers-in-the-uk .html – accessed 14 May 2013).

30. D. Hirsch. 2013. *An Estimate of the Cost of Child Poverty in 2013*, p. 4. Joseph Rowntree Foundation.

31. J. Griggs and R. Walker. 2008. *The Costs of Child Poverty for Individuals and Society: A Literature Review*. Joseph Rowntree Foundation.

32. Op. cit., Aldridge et al. (2013), p. 78.

33. Ibid., p. 86.

34. Ibid., p. 90.

35. Poverty Site, 2011 (http://www.poverty.org.uk/62/index.shtml – accessed 11 June 2013).

36. Marmot Review. 2010. *Fair Society, Healthy Lives: The Marmot Review*, Executive Summary, p. 10.

37. Ibid., p. 12.

38. J. Aber, N. Bennett, D. Conley and J. Li. 1997. The effects of poverty on child health and development. *Annual Review of Public Health* 18:463–483. In D. Hirsch. 2008. *Estimating the Costs of Child Poverty*, p. 6. Joseph Rowntree Foundation.

39. Op. cit., Hirsch (2008), p. 6.

40. D. Caplovitz. 1967. *The Poor Pay More: Consumer Practices of Low-Income Families*. Free Press.

41. A. Westlake. 2010. *The UK Poverty Rip-Off: The Poverty Premium*, p. 1. Save the Children.

42. Trouble on the estate (www.bbc.co.uk/iplayer/episode/b01mqv hs/Panorama_Trouble_on_the_Estate/ – 44 minutes – accessed 18 May 2013).

43. C. Kober. 2008. Why money matters: family income, poverty and children's lives. In *The Poverty Premium* (ed. J. Strelitz and R. Lister), p. 63. Save the Children.

44. S. Bushe, P. Kenway and H. Aldridge. 2013. *The Impact of Localising Council Tax Benefit*, p. 1. Joseph Rowntree Foundation.

45. A. Milne and D. Rankin. 2013. *Reality, Resources, Resilience: Regeneration in a Recession*, p. 12. Joseph Rowntree Foundation.

46. B. Tunstall. 2009. *Communities in Recession: The Impact on Deprived Neighbourhoods: Round-up.* Joseph Rowntree Foundation.

47. A. Hastings, G. Bramley, N. Bailey and D. Watkins. 2012. *Serving Deprived Communities in a Recession.* Joseph Rowntree Foundation.

48. Op. cit., Clery et al. (2013), p. 12.

49. DWP. 2013. *Low-Income Dynamics 1991–2008 (Great Britain).* Department for Work & Pensions.

50. Iain Duncan Smith to Centre for Social Justice (2009).

51. T. Shildrick et al. 2012. *Are 'Cultures of Worklessness' Passed Down the Generations?* Joseph Rowntree Foundation.

52. Op. cit., Clery et al. (2013), p. 22.

53. DWP. 2013. *Public Views on Child Poverty: Results from the First Polling Undertaken as Part of the Measuring Child Poverty Consultation.* Department for Work & Pensions.

54. S. Harkness et al. 2012. *Poverty: The Role of Institutions, Behaviours and Culture,* p. 32. Joseph Rowntree Foundation.

55. Benefits in Britain: separating the facts from the fiction. *The Guardian,* 6 April (www.guardian.co.uk/politics/2013/apr/06/welfare -britain-facts-myths – accessed 11 June 2013).

56. J. Chapman. 2013. Benefit conman who's like Andy in Little Britain: A BENEFITS cheat who claimed he was confined to a wheelchair was secretly filmed walking around a city centre. *The Express,* 15 February. See also J. Delingpole. 2012. There really are far, far too many people sponging off the taxpayer right now with their fake or exaggerated disabilities. *Daily Telegraph,* 26 January.

57. DWP. 2013. *Fraud and Error in the Benefit System: Preliminary 2012/13 Estimates (Great Britain),* p. 15. Department for Work & Pensions.

58. DWP. 2013. *Levelling the Tax Playing Field: Compliance Progress Report,* p. 2. Department for Work & Pensions.

59. Op. cit., Clery et al. (2013), p. 36.

60. D. K. Goodwin. 2005. *Team of Rivals: The Political Genius of Abraham Lincoln.* New York: Simon & Schuster.

61. R. Walker. 2012. Poverty in global perspective: is shame a common denominator. *Journal of Social Policy* 42(2):224. The study looks at rural Uganda, India, urban China, Pakistan, South Korea, small town and urban Norway and the United Kingdom.

62. B. Baumberg, K. Bell and D. Gaffney. 2012. *Benefits Stigma in Britain*, pp. 4–5. Turn2us.

63. Op. cit., Walker (2012), p. 227.

64. J. Strelitz and R. Lister (eds). 2008. *Why Money Matters*, pp. 118, 123. Save the Children.

65. Op. cit., Walker (2012), p. 229.

66. J. G. Stedman. 1971. *Outcast London.* Oxford: Clarendon Press.

67. T. Hobbes. 2008 (originally published: 1651). *Leviathan*, Part II, Chapter 30, p. 255. New York: Simon & Schuster.

68. G . Gilbert. 1997. Adam Smith on the nature and causes of poverty. *Review of Social Economy* LV(3):1.

69. A. Smith. 1776. *An Enquiry into the Nature and Wealth of Nations*, Book 5, Chapter 2.

70. Z. Bauman. 1998. *Work, Consumerism and the New Poor.* Open University Press.

71. P. Butler. 2013. Fear of poverty: just like it was in 1912?, *The Guardian*, 24 August (www.guardian.co.uk/society/patrick-butler-cuts-bl og/2012/aug/24/salvation-army-fear-of-poverty-just-like-1912 – accessed 9 June 2013).

72. C. Moran. 2012. The way I see it (http://esthernagle.tumblr.com/ post/16997915032/caitlin-moran-on-a-childhood-on-benefits – accessed 6 November 2013).

73. Plato. *The Republic*, Book IV: Adeimantus–Socrates.

74. L. Morris. 1994. *Dangerous Classes: The Underclass and Social Citizenship*, p. 2. London: Routledge.

75. Fear of the poor (www.herinst.org/BusinessManagedDemocracy/culture/wealth/fear.html – accessed 13 June 2013).

76. The Charity Organisation Society (www.stgite.org.uk/media/cos .html – accessed 13 June 2013).

77. J. K. Galbraith. 1992. *The Culture of Contentment*, p. 38. London: Penguin.

78. P. L. Wachtel. 1989. *The Poverty of Affluence: A Psychological Portrait of the American Way of Life,* p. 245. Philadelphia, PA: New Society Publishers.

79. T. Jones. 1980. Pressure mounting for public inquiry into Bristol riot. *The Times,* 5 April. Also J. Young. 1980. Anger over unemployment at root of Bristol riot, council chief says. *The Times,* 8 July.

80. K. Clarke. 2011. Punish the feral rioters, but address our social deficit too. *The Guardian,* 5 September.

81. Poverty and wealth across Britain 1968 to 2005 (www.jrf.org.uk/publications/poverty-and-wealth-across-britain-1968-2005 – accessed 6 November 2013).

82. Disability Hate Crime (http://disabilityhatecrime.org.uk/dhc-facts-figures/ – accessed 9 June 2013).

83. Discrimination increases on back of 'benefit scroungers' rhetoric (www.scope.org.uk/news/disability-2012/discrimination – accesed 9 June 2013).

84. Op. cit., Aldridge et al. (2012), p. 86.

85. Investigation of data relating to blind and partially sighted people in the Quarterly Labour Force Survey: October 2009–September 2012 (www.rnib.org.uk/aboutus/Research/reports/2013/Labour_Force_Survey_Report_for_RNIB_OCT_2009-SEPT_2012.doc – accessed 9 June 2013).

86. Jenny Morris reiterates the question asked by Zoe Williams (*Guardian* columnist) (24 May 2013) (http://jennymorrisnet.blogspot.co.uk/2013_05_01_archive.html – accessed 9 June 2013).

87. Working for a healthier tomorrow: work and health in Britain (www.gov.uk/government/publications/working-for-a-healthier-tomorrow-work-and-health-in-britain – accessed 6 November 2013).

88. B. Mooney. 2013. The scientific PROOF that sending mothers out to work harms children – so why is the Budget penalising those who stay at home? *Daily Mail,* 20 March.

89. S. Doughty. 2013. Working mothers risk damaging their child's prospects, *Daily Mail* (www.dailymail.co.uk/news/article-30342/working-mothers-risk-damaging-childs-prospects.html – accessed 10 June 2013).

90. E. Klein. 2012. Mitt Romney flashback: stay-at-home moms need to learn 'dignity of work', *Washington Post* (www.washington-post.com/blogs/wonkblog/post/mitt-romney-flashback-stay-at-home-moms-need-to-learn-dignity-of-work/2012/04/15/gIQAhmbZJT_blog.html – accessed 10 June 2013).

91. P. Dominiczak and R. Mason. 2013 David Cameron's 'slur' on stay-at-home mothers, *Daily Telegraph* (www.telegraph.co.uk/news/politics/9941492/David-Camerons-slur-on-stay-at-home-mothers.html – accessed 8 July 2013).

92. H. Mulholland. 2012. Iain Duncan Smith targets families of more than two children for benefit cuts, *The Guardian*, 25 October (www.guardian.co.uk/politics/2012/oct/25/iain-duncan-smith-benefit-cuts – accessed 10 June 2013).

93. M. Phillips. 2012. Stop this hysteria! Why should the state pay for women on benefits to have more than two children?, *Daily Mail* (www.dailymail.co.uk/debate/article-2224570/Stop-hysteria-Why-state-pay-women-benefits-children.html – accessed 10 June 2013).

94. D. Martin. 2012. The 190 families with ten children who cost you more than £11 million in benefits A YEAR, *Daily Mail* (www.daily mail.co.uk/news/article-2083998/Benefit-cap-190-families-10-children-cost-taxpayers-11m-A-YEAR.html – accessed 10 June 2013).

95. H. Barnard and C. Turner. 2011. *Poverty and Ethnicity: A Review of Evidence*. Joseph Rowntree Foundation.

96. B. Athwal, M. Quiggin, D. Phillips and M. Harrison. 2011. *Exploring Experiences of Poverty in Bradford*, p. 37. Joseph Rowntree Foundation.

97. H. Beider. 2011. *White Working Class Views of Neighbourhood, Cohesion and Change*. Joseph Rowntree Foundation.

98. A. Milne and D. Rankine. 2013. *Reality, Resources, Resilience: Regeneration in a Recession*, p. 14. Joseph Rowntree Foundation.

99. K. Day. 2009. *Communities in Recession: The Reality in Four Neighbourhoods*, p. 13. Joseph Rowntree Foundation.

100. E. Batty and I. Cole. 2010. *Resilience and the Recession in Six Deprived Communities: Preparing for Worse to Come?*, p. 43. Joseph Rowntree Foundation.

101. A. Power, J. Ploger and A. Winkler. 2010. *Phoenix Cities: The Fall and Rise of Great Industrial Cities*. Joseph Rowntree Foundation & Policy Press.

102. Op. cit., Batty and Cole (2010), p. 36.

103. YouGov/Prospect Survey Results, p. 3 (http://cdn.yougov.com/cumulusuploads/document/x3d4a39z0a/YG-Archives-Prospect-Results-welfareReform-120130.pdf – accessed 11 June 2013).

104. P. Gregg, A. Hurrell and M. Whittaker. 2012. *Creditworthy: Assessing the Impact of Tax Credits in the Last Decade and Considering What This Means for Universal Credit*, p. 12. Resolution Foundation.

105. Ibid., p. 47.

106. Ibid., p. 41.

107. N. O'Brien. 2011. *Just Deserts? Attitudes to Fairness, Poverty and Welfare Reform*, p. 1. Policy Exchange.

108. Ibid., p. 16.

109. George Osborne's speech to the Conservative conference (full text via http://www.newstatesman.com/blogs/politics/2012/10/george-osbornes-speech-conservative-conference-full-text – accessed 11 June 2013).

110. S. Crossley. 2013. North East Racial Equality Conference 2013 (http://northeastchildpoverty.wordpress.com/ – accessed 11 June 2013).

111. Op. cit., Clery et al. (2013), pp. 11–12.

112. DWP. 2006. *Low-Income Dynamics 1991–2004 (Great Britain)*. Department for Work & Pensions.

113. J. Monroe. *A Girl Called Jack* (www.agirlcalledjack.com).

114. K. Franklin. *Benefit Scrounging Scum* (http://benefitscroungingscum.blogspot.co.uk).

115. S. Marsh. *Diary of a Benefit Scrounger* (http://diaryofabenefitscrounger.blogspot.co.uk).

116. S. J. Campbell et al. 2012. *Responsible Reform: A Report on the Proposed Changes to Disability Living Allowance: Diary of a Benefit Scrounger*, p. 5. A report written, researched, funded and supported by sick and disabled people, their friends and carers.

117. S. Babones. 2012. *We Won the War on Poverty, Then Lost the Peace* (11 September). Truth-Out.

118. B. D. Meyer and J. X. Sullivan. 2013. *Winning the War: Poverty from the Great Society to the Great Recession.* National Bureau of Economic Research.

119. J. Cribb, R. Joyce and D. Phillip. 2013. *Living Standards, Poverty and Inequality in the UK 2012*, p. 57. Joseph Rowntree Foundation.

120. R. Joyce and L. Sibieta. 2013. *Labour's Record on Poverty and Inequality.* Institute for Fiscal Studies.

121. Op. cit., Cribb et al. (2013), p. 65.

122. Stewart, K. 2009. 'A scar on the soul of Britain': child poverty and disadvantage under New Labour. In *Poverty, Inequality and Policy Since 1997: Towards a More Equal Society?* (ed. J. Hills, T. Sefton and K. Stewart), p. 58. Bristol: Policy Press.

123. Op. cit., Joyce and Sibieta (2013).

124. T. Sefton. 2009. Moving in the right direction? Public attitudes to poverty, inequality and redistribution. In Hills et al. (2009).

125. Op. cit., Cribb (2012), p. 65.

126. M. Brewer, J. Brown and R. Joyce. 2011. *Child and Working-Age Poverty from 2010 to 2020.* Institute for Fiscal Studies.